GOOD ENOUGH FOR
THE CLIMATE

GOOD ENOUGH FOR THE CLIMATE

THE SURPRISINGLY SIMPLE MATH OF THE PLANET AND INSPIRING STORIES OF ACTION AND INNOVATION

JAMES EARL ANDERSON

NEW DEGREE PRESS

GOOD ENOUGH FOR THE CLIMATE
The Surprisingly Simple Math of the Planet and Inspiring Stories of Action and Innovation

ISBN   978-1-63730-697-0   *Paperback*
         978-1-63730-787-8   *Kindle Ebook*
         979-8-88504-019-8   *Ebook*

Dedication

To my children Colette James, June Naomi, and Lucy Rose.

You are the inspiration for all the good things I try to do.

As we say when we go camping, "leave no trace." Here, now, we must do one better. I hope we do that for you.

XO. Daddy

Contents

DEDICATION 5

INTRODUCTION 9

PART 1. **"WE'RE SCREWED" GET OVER IT** **21**

CHAPTER 1. THE NEED AND THE CALL TO ACTION 25

CHAPTER 2. CARBON DIOXIDE AND CARBON REMOVAL 43

CHAPTER 3. THE MATH IS SIMPLE 55

CHAPTER 4. WE CAN DO THIS 65

PART 2. **PRINCIPLES THAT GET US THERE** **77**

CHAPTER 5. THE SCIENCE OF A BIAS TOWARD ACTION 79

CHAPTER 6. PRINCIPLES OF INNOVATION 87

CHAPTER 7. WE NEED MORE WAYS TO PLUG MONEY
INTO THIS 99

CHAPTER 8. REGULATION PLAYS A BIG ROLE 107

PART 3. **EXISTENCE THEOREMS** **123**

CHAPTER 9. GREEN CARBON 127

CHAPTER 10. BLUE CARBON 143

CHAPTER 11. BLACK CARBON 161

CHAPTER 12. GOLD CARBON 177

CHAPTER 13. ESTIMATION AND VERIFICATION 197

CHAPTER 14. THE ROAD AHEAD 213

ACKNOWLEDGMENTS 221

APPENDIX 225

ENDNOTES 249

Introduction

Good Enough for the Climate

The surprisingly simple math of the planet, and the inspiring stories of action and innovation needed to win the climate fight.

As I write this, there is a daily news drumbeat of the impacts of climate change. For another year, wildfires are setting records in the western US. Flooding and heatwaves ravaged Europe this summer. Intensified by climate change, Hurricane Ida paved a path of heavy rain and historic flooding from the Gulf Coast to New York City. It's easy to think these problems are new and unprecedented, but as will be illustrated in the following chapters, there are amazing stories of people who have been working on these issues for decades.

Ricardo Bayon has been working on climate policy and finance since before climate change was a big public issue. He puts you at ease when you speak with him. He's kind and thoughtful. In 1992, Ricardo was working on one of the first climate treaties ratified at the Rio Earth Summit—fourteen years before Vice President Gore's climate documentary, *An Inconvenient Truth*, came out in 2006 and popularized (or demonized) the climate issue for many (Guggenheim 2006).

After helping launch and manage Ecosystem Marketplace, Ricardo and his business partner founded EKO Asset Management in 2008 with a plan to enter the European Union Emissions Trading System (ETS). The ETS was born in 2005 to set a price on CO_2 emissions and incentivize big industries to gradually lower their CO_2 output (Ellerman 2007). The ETS was showing promise, and Ricardo and his partner wanted in. They were in London to sign the agreement, pen nearly on paper, when the Lehman Brothers collapse came across the Bloomberg Terminal. The deal was off, and EKO had to pivot fast. They found a solid investment thesis in setting up a Green Carbon Fund to generate carbon credits for the voluntary emissions trading market in the US and, ultimately, for the California Air Resources Board (CARB) cap-and-trade program. At the time, this was a very novel way to pay landowners—in this case, forest owners— for the climate benefits of preserving their forests.

EKO was a success and generated significant returns for investors. The company created carbon credits and put a price on CO_2 emissions. Under CARB's program, significant emitters of CO_2, like large power plants, only have a permit to emit a set amount of CO_2—a cap. If they want to go over that cap, they must offset those emissions by purchasing a certified carbon credit from a company like EKO. It was the early days, and these markets were new. Standards were hard to come by, and they still need improvement today. Yet, these actions in a small way helped create the foundation for rapidly expanding efforts to put a transparent market-based price on CO_2 emissions today.

At around the same time, Chris Adamo was working as a staffer for US Senator Debbie Stabenow. President Obama had just been elected, and there was the feeling a national CO_2 emissions trading scheme would come to fruition. The House of Representatives had passed a cap-and-trade bill, and there was a group of senators building a coalition to pass their own version. Many thought this was a done deal. The land sector—farmers—were brought into the fold with the promise of new revenue streams to support land management practices to protect the environment, sequester CO_2 from the atmosphere, and reduce agriculture's carbon footprint. Like many constituencies, they were disappointed when the bill faded in the drive toward the mid-term elections. Democrats lost big in those elections, and major climate legislation took a back seat for years to come.

In 2011, Stabenow became Chair of the Senate Agriculture Committee, and Chris was appointed Staff Director. As they were working on the Farm Bill, he saw a broad expanse of programs that could be oriented to bring the land sector into the climate fight. The Farm Bill is a river boat full of programs for managing our nation's farms and forests—a $6 billion conservation budget, $30 billion in farm credit, a range of US Forest Service Programs, and more. It wasn't cap-and-trade, but it was a wide array of programs to make progress on reducing greenhouse gas emissions and removing CO_2 from the atmosphere.

Today we see an expansion of this thinking as the Biden administration takes a whole government approach to address climate change. A myriad of executive actions, spending changes, loan guarantees, rule makings, and other policy adjustments at all levels of the federal government— across all agencies— are accelerating and expanding the response to climate change. This is how government works. It's messy and, at times, seems inefficient and incoherent.

Too often, people are looking for that one thing, that perfect thing, to solve the climate crisis, but what would happen if we stopped looking for the dream solution and simply took action? Ricardo's and Chris's stories exemplify the challenges and pivots involved in any innovative endeavor. I set off on a journey to find out what would happen if we just started trying to be *good enough for the climate.*

When Vice President Al Gore published *An Inconvenient Truth,* it was met with deep fear by some and profound skepticism by others. Some thought climate change was an intractable existential crisis, too big and complex for us to solve. Others thought it wasn't a problem at all. How could a group of odorless, colorless gasses that exist in trace concentrations in a vast atmosphere have a significant impact on our lives? Were the dire predictions going to be true? As much as the climate issue was illuminated and brought into public view, skeptics were also empowered.

However, the pursuit of dogged, careful science over decades has taught us better. Since the Industrial Revolution began around 1870, climate change has largely been driven by an increase in the concentration of man-made carbon dioxide

(CO2), methane (CH4), and a host of smaller pollutants in the atmosphere. It is a wickedly vast and complex global problem. It is impacting nearly every aspect of our lives. It threatens the ecosystems and natural processes on which humans depend. This set of facts isn't debatable anymore and hasn't been for a long time. Reversing this trend will be difficult.

We need to completely retool the way we live to avoid the worst climate change impacts. Today we are just getting a little taste of the severe weather impacts that could come. In 2016, I attended a conference of the American Meteorological Society. At a reception, I ended up drinking margaritas with a physicist and climate researcher from Cal Tech, who was also a self-described mixologist (with some surprise, he declared the premix margaritas served to us in plastic cups "not too bad"). He said, almost glibly, he had run the models, and the world's carrying capacity would decline to 2.5 billion people in the next hundred years (there are currently about eight billion humans in the world). That number could certainly be wrong, but it implies a "shit ton" of disruption. It's understandable to think the problem is too big to solve.

At times, it feels like we haven't made much progress. Global concentrations of CO2 in the atmosphere continue to rise. As I write this, they have topped 420 parts per million for the first time (NASA 2019). Only 37 percent of the world's electric supply comes from low-carbon sources (Rhodes 2021). The global pandemic doesn't seem to have slowed the pace of climate change. The cherry blossoms bloomed the earliest they have in 1,200 years in Kyoto. The weakening polar vortex slung freezing temperatures into Texas in

March 2021, collapsing an electric grid that wasn't resilient enough to handle it, causing nearly statewide power outages for a week or more. Sea temperatures and levels are rising. The year 2020, already rife with tribulation, also experienced the worst wildfire season ever recorded in the western United States, and 2021 is headed in the same direction. It's demoralizing. You can feel the tension, the tiredness, and the burnout.

However, today there is renewed momentum. As I write this, Earth Day has arrived. From a policy perspective, the Biden administration is flexing all the tools available to make progress: issuing executive orders, holding a global summit on climate change, making more aggressive decarbonization pledges, and trying to push a climate mitigation-focused infrastructure bill through the narrowest majority in Congress. Momentum within the private sector is proliferating. Numerous prominent companies are making "net-zero pledges"—the commitments to eliminate or offset emissions from their operations by set dates. General Motors has announced it will stop making internal combustion engines by 2035 (Yurkevich 2021).

I believe we are making more progress than it might seem and that even though the progress may be halting at times, the compounding impact of this progress results in considerable gains as we move forward. In writing this book, I encountered remarkable people, such as Ricardo and Chris, who are innovating with creative solutions, experimenting, and pivoting across many different fields of endeavor to mitigate climate change.

My big idea, and it may be heretical, is "we got this." It will be immensely difficult and will cost way more than we are currently dedicating to the task. But we have the knowledge and the resources to mitigate climate change, avert the worst of its effects, heal our ecosystems, and create better-adapted, more resilient communities to take us into the next century and beyond. I think there are principles of action and innovation that can guide us along the way. I believe there are loads of inspiring stories that show us how it can be done.

Finally, I think we are at the cusp of a broad reshaping of our view toward the natural environment and our place in it. Our efforts to address climate change can foster the formation of a new environmental awareness that brings the value of our ecosystems into the mainstream as never before.

In *Enlightenment Now,* Steven Pinker makes a compelling case for optimism. He points out progress quickly hides its tracks. Our reference point changes as we make progress. What once seemed impossible becomes possible, and we promptly forget all the incremental steps that got us there. Change is also not a gradual or linear process. Over and over again, we see that change comes slow, then fast. As threshold conditions are met, significant changes occur rapidly. If you gradually increase the temperature of a block of ice, it doesn't slowly melt. It all melts once you exceed 0 degrees Celsius. Over the last decade or more, the proportion of electricity generated from low-carbon sources has only increased a few percent. However, we've only recently reached a threshold where the cost of renewable power from wind and solar is on par with or cheaper than coal. Only recently have we begun to internalize the environmental cost of sequestering the CO_2 from burning the coal. This will make the math even more favorable.

Many have convinced themselves the problem is impenetrably complex and huge. On the contrary, the math of climate change is not that complicated, and it's largely incontrovertible. At present, we add about fifty billion tons of CO_2 to the atmosphere each year, according to the Intergovernmental Panel on Climate Change (IPCC). We need to get to zero in thirty years or less to have a decent chance of avoiding the worst impacts of climate change. Large sectors of our economy account for the greatest proportion of emissions. Manufacturing is responsible for 31 percent. Energy production accounts for 27 percent. There is 19 percent that comes from growing things, mostly for food, forage, and fuel. Transportation covers 16 percent. The last 7 percent is for heating and cooling buildings (Gates 2021).

The first step is to electrify everything and stop using fossil fuels to create electricity. We know how to do this. Most of the technology and infrastructure necessary to get this done is in large-scale use today. It will be expensive and burdensome. We will get things wrong, and some stuff won't work along the way. We will have to learn, pivot, and try again. More action needs to be taken, and the pace of change needs to accelerate. We'll need to spend a lot more money and redirect an entire financial system to do so. Electrifying everything also takes care of most of the emissions in the transportation sector as well. Cars, delivery vehicles, most trucks, and all urban transportation can be electrified. Electrification could also decarbonize heating and cooling buildings.

Adoption of regenerative agriculture and forestry practices can greatly reduce CO_2 output from growing food, and in many cases, create positive carbon sequestration benefits. Electrifying transportation means we need less ethanol, thus fewer acres of corn and less of the fossil fuels used for synthetic fertilizer and tractors.

Manufacturing stuff is the hardest part. Whether it's manufacturing concrete or making steel, there are many processes that create CO_2 and other greenhouse gases—this creates a fantastic opening for innovation. New forms of manufacturing and recycling materials can lead to significant reductions in emissions. We will also have to develop and rapidly adopt better ways to capture the CO_2 generated from these processes and sequester it for the long term.

In all areas where emissions can't be cut to zero, we need to put a price on those emissions sufficient to offset them through removal and sequestration. Much of this sequestration will necessarily be from nature-based sources. The oceans hold immense potential for more significant sequestration. Protecting our ecosystems and preserving more land and ocean areas could balance our carbon budget and bring those 50 billion tons to zero or negative. One exceptional attribute of conservation-based solutions is that, in many cases, they are inexpensive and low-tech. Preserving land (mainly leaving it alone), planting trees on a large scale, and preserving large swaths of the ocean doesn't require tons of investment in new technology development and scale-up. The challenging part is measuring the benefits. Nature is vast and complex. It doesn't give up its secrets easily.

Getting all this done will be challenging, but the large-scale math is well established and simple. Many of the solutions exist—and with hard work, ingenuity, and massive investment, we can get there. Our bias should be toward action. Momentum creates its own success.

So why pay attention to me? It's a fair question. I can say this book was fueled by an interest in and passion for the natural world that I've felt since the first time I climbed (and fell out of) a tree in Madison, Wisconsin. I've studied and been around environmental policy and economics most of my adult life. Spending three weeks paddling through Ontario with the Voyageur Outward Bound School, studying ornithology in the Zoology Department and environmental policy in the Department of Environmental Studies at the University of Wisconsin, and working as a research assistant at the Aldo Leopold Reserve near Portage, Wisconsin, have all been seminal experiences that long ago fell off my resume. Working at Earth Networks and now Advanced Environmental Monitoring (AEM), I found a professional setting that married my interest in business with environmental science, economics, and public policy. It's that combination of experiences I bring to this effort. I've trained this base of knowledge, along with curiosity and a genuine desire to better understand these issues, to help mitigate climate change in a way that enriches the biome on which we depend, here in our little spaceship Earth.

This book is for curious and, I hope, some skeptical folks who want to learn more about the stories of people trying to address the climate crisis. It's also for the entrepreneurs, investors, policy makers, and advocates looking for ideas on how to accelerate the vast array of initiatives and changes underway to reshape our economy and how we interact with the natural world to make it more sustainable. In particular, Part 2 outlines principles I think can help us make faster progress, and Part 3 tells numerous stories of the inspiring work being done to increase the rate of change. I hope it spurs loads of creative thought about potential approaches to climate change mitigation. There are so many avenues for productive endeavors that can have a wholly positive impact on this problem. There is room for the first climate trillionaire and many millions of entrepreneurs, investors, advocates, policy makers, scientists, engineers, field technicians, and many, many more to have an impact in this area. In fact, it's axiomatic that for us to meet this challenge, this must be true. The scale of the endeavor requires it.

I hope this book accomplishes a couple of things. First, I hope it's as fun to read as it was to write. I can honestly say it's been surprisingly and incredibly enjoyable. I'm immensely grateful for the opportunity. Writing this book has been a personal revelation. Second, I hope it provides a positive view of our future and our ability to solve this problem. I don't mean a Pollyannish or naive one. This is *hard*. We need vast investment and more ingenuity than ever before. It's a complete retooling of the economy and the built world and a reinvention of how we interact with the natural world (let's stop pretending they are separate things). Without hope, there will be no action. The solutions are there for us to realize it. *We got this.*

PART 1

"WE'RE SCREWED" GET OVER IT

"Peace of mind is rarely found in a past remembered or a future imagined. Instead, it's found in the existence of this very moment and our willingness to embrace it."
—ANDY PUDDICOMBE, HEADSPACE

In many ways, this is a time for calm, not for being blasé. We've got serious work ahead. It will require calmness, creativity, and even some fun to get through this to a better world. Talking about climate change and the corresponding mitigation challenges gets really stressful, really fast. It's a crisis. It's a catastrophe. We can't fix it. It's too big. It's too complex. It will cost too much. Nature is irrevocably ruined. All of this is true, and none of it is. This stress can paralyze us. Yet, there is so much we can do. If we stay here in this moment and focus on the real, implementable solutions around us and take action, we can accomplish a great deal.

The challenge is huge, and we don't have a lot of time. We must rework most of our economy, the way we live, and a good chunk of our built world to fully address climate change. Yet many of the solutions are available to us today at scale.

The situation is too complex. The dynamics of the carbon cycle and how it impacts the climate over long stretches of time are complicated and have significant uncertainty. The science is not perfect. Science is a process and a methodology, not a destination. However, it's pretty darn good. Thousands of people have been studying our climate for decades, and we know enough about the magnitude and direction of change and what's causing it to take meaningful action.

Nature will be *fine* (Stager 2012). It's been through worse and recovered. It doesn't need homo sapiens, but we must take care of it a lot better if we want its cooperation in maintaining this fantastic home for us while we corkscrew through the Milky Way Galaxy at 490,000 mph (Herman 1998). We must come to terms with this fact in a way we never have before. It's not just a new environmental consciousness or ethic like those posited by Muir, Thoreau, or my personal favorite, Aldo Leopold. We need an active, transparent, seamless system to fully account for the benefits nature provides toward human prosperity. As I will say throughout the book, our head and our heart must come together.

Humans are immensely creative and industrious. That's how we got into this mess in the first place. These same qualities can get us out of it—if we choose.

So, we are here, at this moment. It's the only one we have. It's the only thing that matters. What would we like to do with it?

CHAPTER 1

The Need and the
Call to Action

———

"Oh Boy. This Earth is Ruined!"
— TINA FEY (PLAYING LIZ LEMON)

Does anyone remember the show *30 Rock*?

In an episode from season two (airing in 2006), the GE corporate brass is trying to green up its image, so they hire Greenzo, an environmental pitchman played by David Schwimmer, to promote GE products as environmentally friendly. The combination doesn't go well. In the final scene, Greenzo gets into a fight with Jack, the GE executive played by Alec Baldwin, and wrestles for the smiley-faced earth in front of an audience of kids. The earth doesn't fare so well in this battle between the corporate titan and the environmentalist. It bursts into flames when caught in the stage lighting (the sun), and Liz Lemon deadpans, "Oh Boy. This Earth is Ruined!"

The whole episode takes well-deserved potshots at how society views environmental issues. Greenzo is going around acting arrogant, mercilessly criticizing everyone, and pissing them off. At one point, the actress Cerie, played by Katrina Bowden, exclaims, "He just treated me like I wasn't pretty."

It's all a brilliant and thinly veiled dig on our relationships with each other when it comes to climate change. Corporations don't give a crap, or worse, they cynically greenwash their business. Environmentalists are obnoxious, judgmental do-gooders. The general public is too self-absorbed to be bothered. The earth is hopelessly ruined. There is an uncomfortable element of truth to all of this.

Fortunately for us, it's not all true. We've become much more sophisticated about these issues. Opinions about climate change have evolved. We see its impacts more clearly now. Significant action is being taken. For example, when this *30 Rock* episode aired, the European Union Emissions Trading

System was only a year old. Today, we have emissions trading systems covering most of the developed world, including China. We are making progress in many areas, but we have much work to do.

Let's be clear. The problem is *enormous*. We are running short on time. The impacts are real and mounting. Our heads and our hearts must work together on this. We *can* (*we must*) do this.

THE PROBLEM IS HUGE—MATH OF THE PLANET

I'm going to assume we've all gotten over the fact humans are causing climate change. As my fourteen-year-old middle daughter would say, "Facts!" These days, they use the word like my generation used "Duh!" when I was her age. I'm encouraged by this change in vernacular. It feels like a counter to the post-factual era of public discourse in which we live. We need a lot more facts to help get us out of this mess.

In any case, our modern lifestyle causes us to emit gigatons upon gigatons (a gigaton is one billion tons) of CO_2 and lesser quantities of methane (CH_4) and other greenhouse gases into the atmosphere. The chemical structure of these molecules makes them great at trapping energy from the sun in the atmosphere as heat. Slowly, but now more rapidly, the average temperature of the Earth is rising. The year 2020 was the warmest on record. Regional and seasonal differences in this heating create all kinds of impacts that aren't good for the human habitation of the planet. The weather becomes more volatile. They effectively lower the biome's ability to support human life—the planet's carrying capacity. This is all immensely complex. I don't mean to gloss over the details, and more will be covered in Chapters 2 and 3. However, for many actions we need to take, this basic narrative is all that's necessary. Enough said, "Facts! Daddy."

The high-level math of the planet is not complicated or the subject of much debate at this point. To understand just how big the problem is, let's review a few basic numbers. Here I'll focus on CO_2 since it's the most significant greenhouse gas (GHG) and the biggest contributor to climate change. About 60 percent of the greenhouse effect can be attributed to CO_2 (IPCC 2013). It's also the most challenging to regulate. Unlike many other gases that contribute to global warming and climate change, we need CO_2. We produce it. Trees use it. It's the primary means by which carbon, the most essential of all elements, is circulated through our biome. It's also fair to say that if we take care of CO_2, we have, in turn, taken care of a lot of the methane problem, too. If we stop burning fossil fuels, including natural gas, a significant source of methane gets eliminated.

To make the math simple, I'm going to use round numbers. The exact numbers are estimates, and you will see fairly tight ranges referenced in different reports. Simple is good enough and easier to understand. Since the industrial revolution began, we've put about 1.2 trillion tons of CO_2 into the atmosphere (NASA 2019). It lasts for about a thousand years, so most of it is still there. Humans add about another fifty billion tons of CO_2 to this total each year. To prevent the worst impacts of climate change, we must do two things. First, we must eliminate the fifty billion tons of CO_2 we add each year and stop the bleeding, but that's not enough. The world will continue to get hotter and hotter if we don't reduce the concentration of CO_2 in the atmosphere. Currently, all that CO_2

adds up to about 420 parts per million in the atmosphere. That means about .042 percent, less than half of 1 percent of the atmosphere, is made up of CO_2 (NASA 2019—see the composition of the atmosphere below). We need to reduce that significantly, by about half, to "stabilize" the climate around something that most of us would think of as "normal."

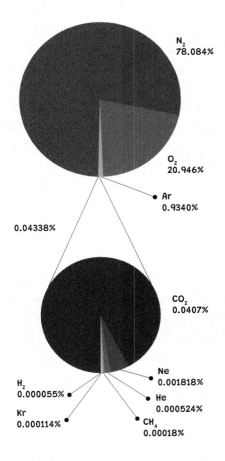

The Composition of the Atmosphere. The Very Tiny Important Parts.

In contrast, other significant GHGs are not naturally occurring or a currency of exchange in the biome. Hydrofluorocarbons (HFCs), ozone in the lower atmosphere, and soot (tiny particles of carbon) are all largely anthropogenic. Even methane, though it is a byproduct of decomposition and ruminant digestion, still has a much easier path to trace in the biosphere. Thus, these GHGs are much easier to source, trace, and regulate. Regulatory systems like the Ozone Treaty and the cap-and-trade system for sulfur dioxide and nitrogen oxide could be applied in these cases. This was the premise of the recent book by Alan Miller called *Cut Super Climate Pollutants Now!* More aggressively regulating these chemicals in the short term could significantly impact the trajectory of our climate, especially in the near term. Alan Miller is a friend and colleague, and I wish I could do his work justice here in this book, but he already wrote a book on it, and I'm obsessed with CO_2 not methane.

Now there is tons of detail, variability, and uncertainty around this, the long-term impacts, changes in sea levels, polar ice packs, surface albedo, and much more. Suffice to say, none of it matters for the decisions we make and the things we need to do right now. Directionally, those details don't impact most of the decisions we need to make. As Cody Simms, senior vice president at Techstars, put it when I asked him about his inspiration to work on climate change issues, "I came to the realization climate change was this huge looming thing I'd read a lot about, and had some cursory understanding of, but hadn't fully stopped to contemplate how much it was going to affect the entire global economy." We'll fill in the gaps in Cody's leap of intuition as we move through the following chapters. The risk of indecision and delay is far greater than the uncertainty in the numbers and climate modalities. The climate change-induced impacts we see today and predict are real, immense, and costly.

THE IMPACTS ARE MOUNTING AND REAL

Many impacts of climate change are already being felt, and the worst of the predicted scenarios are dire. Depending on where you live, what you do, and the things you love, different impacts may feel more significant to you. The impacts will not be distributed evenly. Some communities or regions will be spared. Some communities have more resources to adapt and are more climate-resilient. Wealthier people will, and already are, faring better. We tend to think this stuff won't happen to us. It's tough to see the direct cause and effect on a day-to-day basis. At a personal level in the US, here are some climate change impacts most of us can expect—and are probably feeling today:

1. More damage to your home. We are already having more heavy rain events and more droughts, which means more floods and fires.
2. More expensive insurance. As risks of property damage increase, insurance rates are going up, or insurance is becoming unavailable. Insurance rates in flood- and fire-prone areas are increasing faster.
3. Outdoor work and recreation limits. Heat stress is becoming a greater problem. This impacts food supply chains, construction, and other activities, increasing costs and limiting our movements.
4. Higher electric bills and more blackouts. Heatwaves stress electrical grids, increasing demand and stressing network

operations. The increased frequency of severe weather will cause more power outages. To respond, utilities must reinforce their grid infrastructure and spend more on outage management.

5. Rising taxes. Municipalities are spending more money on infrastructure to address climate change impacts.

6. More allergies, diseases, and other health impacts. As temperatures rise, pollen and mold seasons grow longer and more severe. The range of tropical diseases covers a great proportion of the population. Heat stress and other impacts increase.

7. Food costs rise. Availability and quality decrease. Climate change impacts pollinators that are necessary for 75 percent of our crops. More severe weather will make growing seasons less predictable. Costs of adaptation will be borne by this sector and passed on to consumers.

8. Water quality and supply diminishes. Excessive runoff from severe storms can pollute streams and lakes. This surface water is the supply for municipal water systems. Sea level rise will inundate coastal groundwater supplies with saltwater.

9. Travel and recreation become harder. More delays and disruptions due to severe weather. Fewer days and places where we can spend time outside.

All of this might seem like nuisance-level stuff, especially if you have the means to adapt. You can spend the money necessary to overcome most of these issues or move. If you are on the margins, though, these impacts can be a substantial hardship. The effects of climate change are not felt equally. It's already impacting property values disproportionately.

When we add up these risks, they become much more significant global problems.

GLOBAL RISKS

The consensus around the global risks of climate change is stunning at times. Each year, the World Economic Forum, a renowned non-government organization, conducts analysis on global issues related to human thriving, engages with business leaders, politicians, and academics on these subjects, and puts out a Global Risks Report. Climate Change and climate-related risks have been topping the list for years, and that consensus is growing. It's staggering to see the shift over time. The chart below shows the top ten risks by likelihood and impact. You can see how environmental risks have grown to dominate the analysis over the last fourteen years.

TOP GLOBAL RISKS

From economic to environmental. Climate now tops the risks agenda, while the economy has disappeared from the top five.

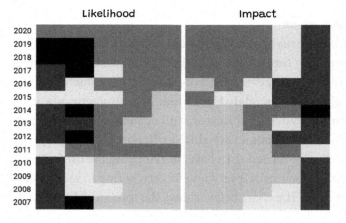

	Likelihood	Impact
2020		
2019		
2018		
2017		
2016		
2015		
2014		
2013		
2012		
2011		
2010		
2009		
2008		
2007		

Economic

Asset bubble
Critical infrastructure failure
Deflation
Energy price shock
Financial failure
Fiscal crises
Illicit trade
Unemployment
Unmanegeavle inflation

Environmental

Biodiversity loss
Climate action failure
Extreme weather
Human-made environmental disaster
Natural disasters

Geopolitical

Global governance failure
Interstate conflict
National governance failure
State collapse
Terrorist attacks
Weapons of mass destruction

Societal

Failure of urban planning
Food crises
Infectious diseases
Involuntary migration
Social instavility
Water crises

Technological

Adverse technological advances
Cyberattacks
Data fraud or theft
Information infrastucture breakdown

Here you can see the top ten risks over the next ten years, five of which are environment or climate-related. If you accept that water crises and infectious diseases are also heavily influenced by climate change, it's really seven of ten.

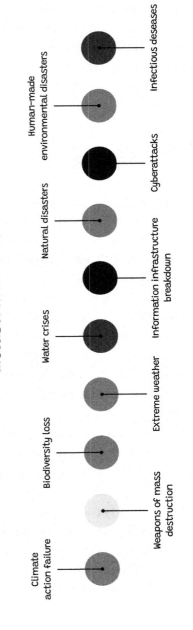

TOP 10 RISKS OVER THE NEXT 10 YEARS

Long-Term Risk Outlook: Impact

Multistakeholders

Climate action failure

Weapons of mass destruction

Biodiversity loss

Extreme weather

Water crises

Information infrastructure breakdown

Natural disasters

Cyberattacks

Human-made environmental disasters

Infectious deseases

Economic   Environmental   Geopolitical   Societal   Technological

These environmental risks are not coming *from* the environment. They are the result of our activities. The US is not immune to this. The impacts here are detailed in national climate assessments that are done every four years (USGCRP 2018). The last one was in 2018.

IMPACTS IN THE US

The US National Climate Assessment states, "The impacts and costs of climate change are already being felt in the US, and changes in the likelihood or severity of some recent extreme weather events can now be attributed with increasingly higher confidence to human-caused warming." The costs of these events are increasing. Events such as Hurricane Harvey, which caused massive damage along the coast of Texas, are made more frequent (Dunne 2017). The National Oceanic and Atmospheric Administration (NOAA) concluded there were twenty-two such events—a new record—in 2020, and the number and cost of these disasters have been increasing (Smith 2021). We see the impacts all around us today. The 2020 fire season in the west has been followed by another very severe season in 2021. A "mega-drought" has been declared throughout the western US. A heatwave across the Pacific Northwest brought record temperatures, which many believed weren't possible. These extreme weather events have spawned a new type of forensic weather analysis called "climate attribution science." Investigators are now looking at individual severe weather events to estimate how much more likely these events are due to climate change.

NATIONAL SECURITY

So what happens, for example, when flooding and sea-level rise causes fifty million Bangladeshis to seek higher ground in India or China? That might be horribly destabilizing for the region and beyond. It was grain shortages caused by a succession of climate-induced poor wheat harvests that contributed to the onset of the Arab Spring. The refugee crisis that followed engulfed much of Europe.

The Pentagon has identified climate change as a national security priority, and a 2019 report by the Department of Defense examined the impact of climate change on military activities (Mehta 2021; DOD 2019). The department itself has an emissions footprint comparable with a medium-sized country (Crawford 2019).

The threats the military has highlighted include desertification, crop failure, famine, destabilizing societies, and melting ice opening up new routes to the US through the Arctic. This is where the list of seemingly nuisance-level impacts above becomes potentially catastrophic and destabilizing.

THE DETAILED MATH IS FUZZY, AND THAT'S OKAY RIGHT NOW

Given the risks and implications, how do we establish clear goals for CO_2 emissions reductions and track our progress and the efficacy of different mitigation efforts? The detailed measurement, reporting, and verification of the carbon sequestration benefits of various actions is problematic and has been fraught with high-profile errors, but that shouldn't stop us. As Eric Letsinger, the CEO of Quantified Ventures, put it, "It's early innings. We know we must improve our measurement, reporting, and verification (MRV). Everything about the transparency and accuracy of these types of programs must improve, and it is. But we have to start somewhere, and nature-based solutions will be part of the mix".

This is especially challenging for green and blue carbon solutions—the nature-based forestry, agricultural, marshland, tidal, and ocean solutions reviewed in Chapters 9 and 10. An analysis of carbon credits from these types of programs called many of them into question. Yet, the standards are becoming more established and coalescing around solid principles. I explore this in more detail in Chapter 13.

THE HEAD AND THE HEART MUST COME TOGETHER

Part of the solution to getting fifty gigatons of CO_2 emissions to zero and going negative, as we must, is helping the environment—the biome, our ecosystem—to sequester more carbon in long-term storage. To be successful in forestalling the worst impacts of climate change, we must bring our heads and our hearts together. We must come to a complete understanding that we are integral to nature, not separate from it. Everything we do, our economic activity—production, consumption, movement, etc.—all takes place in, is impacted by, and impacts the natural world. There is no *us* and *nature*. We are one big whole. The advent of the climate change issue in the early part of the century created a rift in the environmental community that needs to be reconciled.

The environmental movement was split between the energy- and engineering-oriented camp working on how to reduce CO_2 and other GHG emissions as much as possible. This took focus away from traditional conservation efforts. It became a conflict between the "carbon cowboys" and the "tree huggers." To some extent, this rift still exists today and is counterproductive. The head and the heart must come together. "For too long, we have been waging a senseless and suicidal war on nature," said UN Secretary-General Antonio Guterres at a news briefing. "The result is three interlinked environmental crises: climate disruption, biodiversity loss, and pollution that threaten our viability as a species."

Long-standing, known flaws in our economic system need to be reconciled as part of the path forward. "Economic and financial systems fail to account for the essential benefits that humanity gets from nature and to provide incentives to manage nature wisely and maintain its value... Conventional metrics like gross domestic product (GDP) overstate progress because they fail to adequately capture the costs of environmental degradation or reflect declines in natural capital," (Hu 2021).

Mark Lambert has worked across a couple of different climate mitigation-related startups and is one of the amazing people at the front lines trying to bring our heads and our hearts closer together. For Mark and others, there is no contradiction in applying business and economic principles to addressing these problems. "From my personal career perspective, in any of the projects I'm working on, it's always been about trying to leverage markets to help solve for climate-related challenges. I see markets as an opportunity, rather than just the cause, of many of the environmental challenges we're currently facing" (Lambert 2021). Markets are human contrivances. They should represent our values and generate the outcomes we want, considering all the costs and benefits we choose to include. A free market economy is a phenomenal tool for efficiently applying capital to a problem and creating incentive structures that nudge behavior, so why not make it work for the outcomes necessary to help address climate change, water quality, air quality, or a whole host of ecosystem services?

There may be a path forward to a new environmental awakening that truly mainstreams this notion. The accounting has to be completely integrated and seamless. It has to be pervasive. As Mark put it, "When these markets are harnessed for good, I think there is potential for significant transformative change. That's what I've been trying to focus my career on, predominantly—getting more traditional sources of capital aligned around mitigating climate change." Of course, markets aren't a silver bullet, one-size-fits-all solution, and as the problems get bigger and time gets shorter, we will need to reach for every tool in the shed. Fortunately, a lot of people are.

WE CAN DO THIS (WE MUST)

As I've researched this book, I've encountered an impressive network of intelligent, industrious people with incredible imaginations and the desire to solve these problems. Every day I meet someone who is doing outstanding work and is laser-focused on solving part of the issue. The drive to address the climate crisis is in every corner I look at. Entrepreneurs are launching startups across every sector. Investors are plowing more money into climate-related ventures than ever before. The mainstream financial sector is working to quantify risk, create standards, and push their portfolio companies to decarbonize. Policymakers are pulling all the levers of government to incentivize and accelerate change. Scientists are doggedly pursuing the facts in a highly politicized environment. I started this journey wondering what would happen if we just started taking action, and I think there is immense potential.

OUR CALL TO ACTION

So, it's horrible. The global consensus is this problem is wickedly vast and complex. We need to decarbonize most of our economic activity and our built world. To do this, we are going to need every tool in the chest and every resource available. Our head and our heart must come together. Humans are a bright bunch, and with enough caffeine and hard work, we got this. Let's talk more about the problem and how we solve it.

CHAPTER 2

Carbon Dioxide and Carbon Removal

―――

1995: "The balance of evidence suggests a discernible human influence on global climate."

2001: "There is a new and stronger evidence that most of the warming observed over the last fifty years is attributable to human activities."

2007: "Human-induced warming of the climate system is wide-spread."

2013: "It is extremely likely that human influence has been the dominant cause of the observed warming since the mid-20th century."

2021: "It has been clear for decades that the Earth's climate is changing, and the role of human influence on the climate system is undisputed...human actions still have the potential to determine the future course of the climate."

—IPCC, SECOND, THIRD, FOURTH, FIFTH, AND SIXTH ASSESSMENT REPORTS ON THE CLIMATE.

I love seltzer water. I have one of those Soda Streams in my house so I can have as much of it as I want without the waste of cans and bottles. I guess I love CO_2. That feels confusing. How is it a colorless, odorless gas and a few of its friends that exist at minute trace levels in our atmosphere are pollutants so powerful they could dramatically alter the Earth's climate for thousands of years, making it uninhabitable for humans, and cause a mass extinction of other living things? How is it possible that something essential for life can also, at slightly higher concentrations, be so detrimental to it? How is it possible humans can have such an immense impact on something as vast as the climate? What has led, as we see above, thousands of scientists conducting careful peer-reviewed research over decades to increase the volume and certainty of their alarm?

THE SLOW MARCH OF SCIENCE

Part of what makes this interesting is the story of how we know all this. How did we learn how all the pieces of the puzzle fit together? It's the story of the methodical grind of science over more than two centuries. Like so many basic scientific discoveries, it started with European noblemen and clergy in the eighteenth and nineteenth centuries. It was the Enlightenment. It's amazing how many discoveries from that time we still rely on today. The carbon cycle was first articulated by Antoine Lavoisier, a French nobleman, and Joseph Priestley, a clergyman and teacher. Both studied chemistry. Priestley discovered oxygen. Lavoisier discovered the law of conservation of mass. Many others followed to flesh out the details and helped popularize this description of how carbon flows through our environment. This is just one cornerstone of the science behind global warming and climate change.

Carbon dioxide's heat-trapping powers weren't understood until much later. In the 1850s, Eunice Newton Foote, a thirty-seven-year-old female American physicist, discovered a bottle of CO_2 placed in the sun rose to a higher temperature than that of a bottle filled with air. Other scientists explained the physical properties that caused this effect. Svante Arrhenius was a Swedish physical chemist and Nobel laureate. Amazingly, in the 1890s (yeah, one hundred thirty years ago), he estimated if the CO_2 concentration doubled, the Earth would be four degrees Celsius warmer. Directionally, this is correct. *It's stunning how accurate this was* (Wicks 2020).

In the early twentieth century, Guy Callendar turned his attention to CO_2. In a 1938 paper, he showed fuel burning was adding CO_2 to the atmosphere faster than the carbon cycle could absorb it. He even went so far as to say this would cause an increase in temperature.

Starting in the 1950s, Charles David Keeling began working on the highly accurate measurements you needed to quantify the concentration of CO_2 in the atmosphere. His calculations, running continuously since 1958, have proven what Callender estimated in 1938. The plot of these measurements has been enshrined as the "Keeling Curve." The concentration of CO_2 in the atmosphere continues to rise. About 55 percent of CO_2 from human activity remains in the atmosphere (Neri, 2021). It's been proven this increase in CO_2 concentrations will trap more infrared radiation in the atmosphere, which causes an increase in global temperatures. Further, we can attribute this temperature rise to a variety of global impacts, thanks to high-resolution global-scale models that have been running for decades.

Thousands of scientists have diligently pulled these threads over time, knitting together a clear tapestry today:

- The carbon cycle and our understanding of how carbon moves through the environment
- Properties of CO_2 as an energy trapping gas
- Fuel burning and human activity that produces more CO_2 than the carbon cycle can absorb
- Quantification of rising CO_2 levels as shown by the Keeling Curve
- Quantification of the heat-trapping effects and temperature rise
- Attribution of this temperature rise to changes in our climate and impacts on our environment

These are the building blocks of what we know today and what we see is a huge threat to human thriving. You can't talk about climate change without telling a little bit of this amazing story—thousands of scientists running a massive relay race over centuries to acquire the knowledge and insight we have today. We are lucky to have it.

CARBON—THE BUILDING BLOCK OF LIFE AND THE CARBON CYCLE

It's understandable that we've been perplexed by climate change and the role CO_2 has played in it for so long. If it weren't for the CO_2 in our atmosphere, Earth would be unbearably cold. In the right proportion, the molecules' heat-trapping characteristics prevent just the right amount of the sun's energy from escaping the atmosphere.

Carbon is the building block of life. Every living thing we know is carbon-based. We are about 18 percent carbon. Only oxygen (O_2) makes up a bigger proportion of our mass, and that's because humans are, in essence, big saltwater balloons, and water is mostly oxygen. Carbon has this handy atomic structure that allows it to bond with all kinds of stuff in many different geometric shapes. Broadly speaking, carbon glues together all the other common elements in our environment to make all the cool stuff in our natural world—plants, animals, minerals, enzymes, proteins, viruses, coral reefs, you name it.

All these life forms and physical structures trade carbon with each other. This exchange is called the "carbon cycle," which can be defined as:

"The series of processes by which carbon compounds are inter-converted in the environment, involving the incorporation of carbon dioxide into living tissue by photosynthesis and its return to the atmosphere through respiration, the decay of dead organisms, and the burning of fossil fuels" (Lexico).

The term "carbon cycle," just like "greenhouse effect," is a bit of a misnomer. It's not a cycle as much as a web of stocks and flows of carbon in different forms throughout the Earth's environment. Carbon flows through the air as CO_2. It is dissolved in water. Through these transport mechanisms, it ends up in plants and animals. It gets absorbed by the ocean and transported deep to sediments through an amazing set of interactions and processes. It gets incorporated into the soil as organic matter from plants and other organisms. These are all stocks or stores of carbon that have varying sizes and lengths. A forest may store carbon for fifty or a hundred years. Carbon transported to the bottom of the ocean may stay there for thousands. All of this is all the "fast" carbon cycle. There is also a "slow" geologic cycle where carbon is sequestered in mineral forms or released through volcanic eruptions, ocean floor vents, and so on.

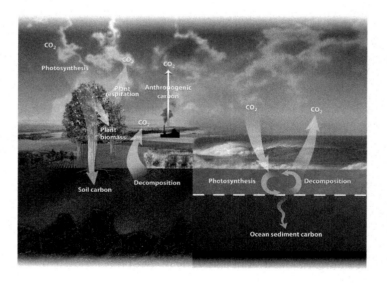

The Carbon Cycle—Fast and Slow

Humans have impacted many of these stocks and flows, so more of the carbon is being stored in the atmosphere as CO_2. Deforestation, extractive agricultural practices, habitat loss, and overfishing reduce the ability of the biome to uptake and store more CO_2 from the atmosphere. Burning fossil fuels oxidizes carbon from long-term storage and tosses it into the atmosphere as CO_2. Chemical processes to make all kinds of stuff we like produce CO_2. One way to think of it is we've taken the slow carbon cycle and accelerated it by turning geologic carbon—oil and coal—into atmospheric CO_2.

On an annual basis, the change doesn't seem to be that big. We are currently adding about two parts per million per year to the global concentration of CO_2 in the atmosphere. CO_2 is tough stuff, though. It doesn't decay naturally very easily, so it can accumulate in the atmosphere for hundreds or thousands of years unless it's processed by photosynthesis or dissolved in the ocean. The result is a gradual accumulation of CO_2 in the atmosphere. Before the industrial revolution, the concentration of CO_2 in the atmosphere was about 280 parts per million. Now, it's over 400, most of the time—almost a 40 percent increase, which represents about 1.2 trillion tons of CO_2. That's a tremendous change (Oceana). Okay, so why is that a big deal?

CARBON DIOXIDE, TRACE GASES, AND THE GREENHOUSE EFFECT

CO_2, at the right level, is excellent stuff. It is the primary way carbon is transported around. All our food and shelter wouldn't be possible if it wasn't for CO_2 making carbon available to grow plants we eat and use to build stuff. CO_2 is also high-energy stuff. It's what keeps us warm. Unlike many molecules in the atmosphere, CO_2 is a little bigger and a little more complex, with a structure that likes to store energy as heat. The IPCC lists about twenty-five gases that contribute to climate change. Water vapor, CO_2, CH_4, and N_2O are the most consequential (IPCC 2013). These gases have something in common: they like to absorb energy. In simple terms, most of the energy that hits the planet comes from the sun as light. That light is absorbed by the surface and reflected out as heat in the infrared spectrum. The bigger molecules of CO_2 and methane are efficient and, in some cases, are extremely good at absorbing light energy as heat. So, these gases don't trap air in a greenhouse per se; they absorb heat, making the atmosphere warmer.

I don't talk a lot about methane (CH_4), but it's worth mentioning here. It's an incredibly potent greenhouse gas. Its chemical structure can absorb a lot of energy, about twenty-five times more than CO_2, and this factor compounds over time. Fortunately, it exists at a small fraction of the concentration as CO_2, and it doesn't stick around nearly as long, but it's a big problem. A lot of it comes from the extraction and transportation of the natural gas we use to power and heat our homes, as feedstock for manufacturing processes, and many other applications. It also comes from animal production. Cows are great at producing the stuff, and humans are great at producing and consuming cows, so that's a problem. Methane is a problem. Fortunately, it's one we can deal with.

To reduce our CO_2 emissions, we will burn a lot less fossil fuel, which means burning less methane. Thus, we'll extract and transport less methane. This change means less leakage into the atmosphere. Much of this is a point source problem as well that is easier to regulate. As for livestock production, there are numerous options for reducing methane emissions. Consuming less beef and changing the way it's produced can significantly lower the methane footprint of this sector. These solutions don't address the entire problem, but they are achievable methods of making significant progress.

Thanks to decades of painstaking and far-reaching research, the math of the planet is not that complicated and, at its core, not controversial. To mitigate climate change, we need to be very numerical about the problem. We must reduce the amount of CO_2 that humans (and all our stuff) emit by about fifty million tons per year. We must partner with nature to improve its health and help it remove more CO_2 from the atmosphere and store it in biomass, soil, sediment, and living things.

THE COLOR OF CARBON

As we can see, carbon in all its forms is this fantastic, dynamic, essential thing. Physically and culturally, carbon takes on many colors. Long before I started this project, I thought it would be powerful to put a color on carbon to show how human activity changes the concentration of CO_2 in real-time. We could make this odorless, colorless gas tangible. Wouldn't it be cool to see a real-time, 3D display of the concentration of carbon in your area and see how it was changing over time?

There is a wonderful article in *Nature Sustainability* that outlines how culturally we've assigned colors to different types of sources and sinks of carbon (Zinke 2020). In chapters to follow, we'll focus on a few colors from that article and a couple more I made up:

Green Carbon—The Land Sector. As I write this, I'm sitting in a wooded area filled with sycamore and tulip poplar trees. The buzzing sound of innumerable Brood X cicadas is all around me. Everything is green and lush. This scene is one pretty nice picture of Green Carbon, but it's everything about how humans interact with, manage, and conserve our land ecosystems, forests, and farms. When they are abundant, healthy, and organized well, they can help restore the right balance to the carbon cycle.

Blue Carbon—The Oceans and Coastal Environment. Our oceans are vast. They are massively productive. They absorb and process more CO_2 than anything. They are also imperiled. Largely outside of regulatory reach, they are hard to manage and conserve. Like the land sector, and likely to a greater degree and faster, their productivity can be improved to fight climate change. We need to leave them alone.

Black Carbon—Engineered Solutions. Humans produce a lot of CO_2 to build and power our world and move around it. We need to find ways to do all that without putting CO_2 into the atmosphere. When we produce electricity, it needs to be done without putting CO_2 into the atmosphere. We must produce concrete, steel, plastic, and glass in ways that don't produce CO_2 as part of the manufacturing process. When we move ourselves or our stuff around, we must do it without burning fossil fuels. All the engineered solutions we need to do this are part of our Black Carbon world. In fact, given how much extra CO_2 we've accumulated in the atmosphere, we need to figure out how to get in a net-negative balance with nature.

Gold Carbon—The Money. Preserving nature and refactoring our built world takes a lot of investment. Trillions of dollars are needed. We need much better incentives as well. It seems like making the world a cleaner, more prosperous place should be profitable. It's our job to make the economy work that way.

In these areas, we can steer the math of the planet in a sustainable direction, preserving nature and ourselves.

CHAPTER 3

The Math Is Simple

"In an earlier draft of this letter, I started this section with arguments and examples designed to demonstrate human-induced climate change is real. But, bluntly, I think we can stop saying that now. You don't have to say photosynthesis is real, or make the case that gravity is real, or that water boils at 100 degrees Celsius at sea level. These things are simply true, as is the reality of climate change."
—JEFF BEZOS, AMAZON 2020 LETTER TO SHAREHOLDERS

As I write this chapter, a court in the Netherlands has just ordered Royal Dutch Shell to more substantially reduce its emissions and those of its products by 2030. ExxonMobil has lost a proxy fight for three members of its board to be replaced by new candidates advocating for more rapid progress on the decarbonization of its business. The same day, a shareholder proposal demanding Chevron more rapidly decarbonize its Scope 3 emissions (these are emissions associated with the use of its products, i.e., burning fossil fuels) passed with over 60 percent of the vote. These giant companies have the most to lose, and one could argue the most to gain (we'll get to that in Chapter 11) from the drive to mitigate climate change (Woellert 2021). Clearly, Mr. Bezos is correct. The math of the planet is not controversial. It's not all that complicated, and it has massive implications. Just ask the CEOs of Shell, Exxon, and Chevron.

This news aside, it seems we've gotten hung up on the math for decades. Even today, with clear signals of the impacts of climate change and its well-established physical underpinnings, there are still skeptics saying the science isn't sound enough and the costs are too high. They say we don't know enough to invest trillions of dollars on a transition away from fossil fuels or the other changes we must make.

Earth systems are complicated, vast, and hard to observe. Ecosystem-level interactions and feedback loops can be hard to understand and model. Nor are they constant and unchanging. Some exchanges are hard to track once, let alone consistently over time. However, the work of the IPCC and thousands of scientists over more than a generation have nailed the big picture down tight. If the facts are clear enough for the investors, boards of directors, and courts overseeing three of the largest companies in the world, shouldn't that math be good enough for the planet? Let's review the math.

THE GLOBAL CARBON BUDGET

The total stock of carbon on earth is essentially fixed. It was the amazing endowment of our planetary beginnings. More than 99 percent of it is locked up under our feet, so we are only concerned with the flux in the carbon cycle, specifically the "fast" carbon cycle that covers seconds to centuries outlined in Chapter 2. More specifically, we are interested in the parts of the carbon cycle altered by humans who have a sizable impact on the concentration of atmospheric CO_2 over the next couple of decades. We'll examine this in Part 3— this narrows down the problem and where we should focus. Whether you are a policymaker, entrepreneur, or investor, understanding the carbon cycle and the levers we can pull is essential. So, here's a summary of that current carbon budget and what drives it.

As described in both the Introduction and Chapter 2, there are several greenhouse gases (GHGs) that are most important. Here I will focus on the granddaddy of them all: CO_2. There are a couple of reasons for doing this. First, the methane problem and the CO_2 problem are intrinsically linked to fuel burning and land use. If we solve for the CO_2 problem, we will ameliorate much of the methane problem. Second, methane and other lesser GHGs are shorter-lived in the environment—they break down. CO_2 can circulate in the atmosphere for a thousand years or more. We must change the dynamics of the carbon cycle to sequester more carbon in the biome and long-term stocks or stores out of the atmosphere. Third, it's the most confounding to regulate. It's as hard to label CO_2 a pollutant as it is water. It's the stuff of life.

With the centuries of research that have preceded, we know a lot about our global carbon budget. We know how much of that budget we can spend before we go into debt. We also know we've been going into debt at an accelerated rate since the Industrial Revolution. We know this because we know the atmospheric concentration of CO_2 has increased rapidly since the Industrial Revolution and has been accelerating further since about 1950. We know this for sure because of the work of many scientists who are extraordinarily good at measuring things and staying at it for their entire careers. As you can see below, CO2 levels have increased steadily from about 280 ppm (parts per million) to about 410 ppm—this is the Keeling Curve referenced in Chapter 2. Keeling not only proved the concentration was increasing but that it was seasonally decreasing as crops and forests began to absorb more CO2 in spring. He also showed the proportion of carbon isotopes associated with fossil fuel burning were increasing in the atmosphere. These discoveries proved humans caused the rise in CO2.

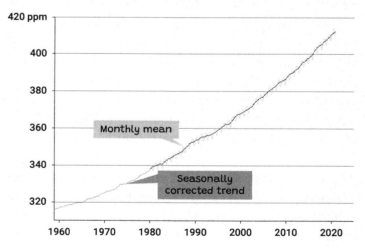

The Keeling Curve

As reviewed in Chapter 2, Guy Callender hypothesized back in 1938 that fuel burning was creating more CO_2 than the carbon cycle could absorb. Today we know this change is mostly from anthropogenic (human-caused) changes in the carbon cycle. Humans rapidly burn fossil fuel or use it in other industrial processes that produce lots of CO_2. We alter land-use patterns on a grand scale that release CO_2. We also contribute to other changes that limit the net sink of those areas. For example, overfishing, bottom trawling, and habitat loss in the oceans likely reduce the amount of CO_2 the oceans can absorb and sequester. Below you can see the major sources and sinks estimated from a variety of source data for 2020 expressed in metric gigatons of CO_2.

Net it all out, and we are adding about twenty-one billion tons of CO_2 to the atmosphere each year, and it stays there for a thousand years. The Keeling Curve will keep marching to the northeast of this now-famous graph. The deficit spending continues, so our debt to the natural world on which we depend continues to grow. Like with all debts, we pay interest. The interest we will pay here is the cost of adaptation, the disruption, all the negative impacts described in Chapter 1, and more.

To get to zero emissions, *we need to eliminate all of the anthropogenic CO_2 produced each year from all of our processes.* Throughout this book, I use the round number of 50 billion tons per year. In the chart below, we can see the inflows and the major sources and sinks—the spending and savings in our budget—since the Industrial Revolution and

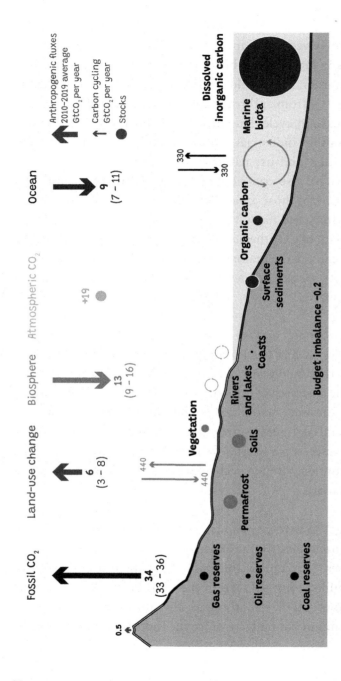

Major Sources and Sinks of Carbon

in the last ten years. The blue bar is what has been added to the atmosphere. It's human-induced emissions the land and sea couldn't absorb through photosynthesis and other processes.[1]

Anthropogenic carbon flows

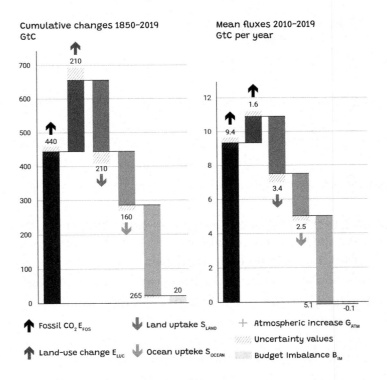

(Global Carbon Project 2020)

Finally, we can see how all of this translates into an increase in the concentration of CO_2 in the atmosphere. The chart below shows how our budget got us from the atmosphere of 1850 to the one we have today.

Sources and Sinks of CO$_2$

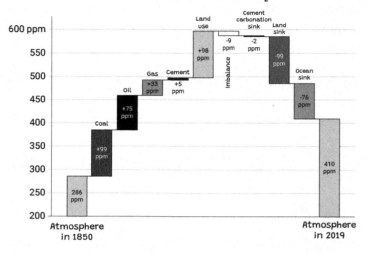

(Global Carbon Project 2020)

Why do we need to get to *zero* emissions, eliminating all anthropogenic sources (about fifty billion tons per year), rather than just get to *net zero*, balancing the budget to include all the natural sinks (about twenty-one billion tons per year)? There are lots of reasons, but there are a couple of biggies. First, to stabilize the climate, we must lower the concentration of CO$_2$ in the atmosphere, and we need to do it quickly. Second, as temperatures continue to rise, it's likely some natural sinks will be compromised. We are seeing this now with melting permafrost, wildfires, and other impacts. Third, as the oceans absorb more carbon, they become more acidic. Through a series of reactions, some of the CO$_2$ creates more carbonic acid. This addition can alter the balance of ocean ecosystems—which, as we will see, are key drivers of the carbon cycle and our carbon budget.

How much deficit spending can we incur before the interest payments get too big to pay? Put another way, how much more CO_2 can we put in the atmosphere before we see catastrophic impacts of climate change that make it very tough for humans?

REMAINING CARBON BUDGET

With the carbon budget nailed down, we can turn to the next critical piece of the puzzle for mitigating climate change. What are the remaining emissions left to limit global warming to an acceptable level? This is the remaining carbon budget, and for this example, I'll use the remaining carbon budget for limiting a rise in global average temperatures to 1.5 degrees Celsius. Current estimates average out that we can add no more than 420 gigatons of CO_2 to the atmosphere to avoid the worst impacts of climate change. This gives us about twenty years to get to zero (Hausfather 2018).

WHAT DOES ALL OF THIS MEAN?

There are a ton of assumptions and estimates in every aspect of this. The global carbon cycle is well understood but also vast and complex. There are many assumptions about land-use patterns, ocean mixing, and on and on. The carbon budget, too, is complex. The exact relationship between CO_2 emissions, concentrations, and warming of surface air temperatures has uncertainty, too. It's easy to get lost in the details, but all this uncertainty and estimation are well understood. We know there may be surprises, and impacts will vary widely. Climate change as a physical phenomenon has been understood for over a hundred years, and we've been modeling all aspects of this rigorously for about fifty years. The basic math and relationships have stood the test of time. Everything clearly points in one direction.

This discussion brings my mind to a more philosophical point. This whole exercise of figuring out the earth's carbon cycle and how it drives global climate regulation will be an ongoing human management challenge forever. We have truly reached the Anthropocene. We live in an epoch where humans control almost everything on a timescale relevant for every living thing on Earth. Most classical science and economics teach us that there are boundary conditions and externalities out of our control or inconsequential to us. That assumption is not just flawed; it's completely erroneous now. Nature needs us to get our shit together, and we need nature if we want to thrive. The head and the heart must come together. Axiomatically, this is *our time*—the Anthropocene, the epoch of humans. What are the principles that drive us to action?

CHAPTER 4

We Can Do This

———

Jim: "Secretary Taalas, you sound optimistic."

Secretary Taalas: "I am. I am! Because I have been following this since the 1980s. The ambition we see to implement the Paris Agreement is a clear signal of change."
—DR. PETERRI TAALAS, SECRETARY-GENERAL OF
THE WORLD METEOROLOGICAL ORGANIZATION

It might be heretical, but it's important to say, "we can do this." It's possible, and in fact necessary, to hold onto that belief while at the same time understanding the extreme gravity and peril of the situation. For there to be action, there must first be hope. The comments from Secretary Taalas are particularly telling. A Finnish scientist by trade, Dr. Taalas isn't one to overestimate things. Through his decades-long experience, he sees progress in the quickening cadence of change and the increasing urgency in the statements of policymakers, officials, and business leaders. He's also quick to point out we don't know what the endpoint will be. There is still plenty of uncertainty in the impacts of climate change, how the biosphere will respond to warming, and how quickly society can reduce emissions. We have a lot of work to do.

Early this year, it was reported that based on the emissions reduction commitments of the 197 countries that have committed to the Paris Agreement, their Nationally Defined Contributions, we only have a 5 percent chance of staying below the 2-degree Celsius target for climate change. Countries needed to increase their commitments by 80 percent to ensure we avoid the worst impacts (Liu 2021).

We are already seeing the increasing impacts of climate change. In 2020, California had the worst wildfire season in history. The rains are coming a month later, and they are now facing drought conditions. In the winter of 2020, a polar vortex caused much of the Texas power grid to collapse. Hurricane Ida rapidly intensified. Its maximum sustained winds increased over 70 mph in less than twenty-four hours in the climate-warmed waters of the Gulf of Mexico before making landfall near New Orleans, sixteen years to the day after Hurricane Katrina. There was record cold across the south. Blue sky flooding is a regular occurrence in southern Florida. We feel the impacts of climate change more frequently, and we more readily associate severe weather with climate change.

Yet progress has already been made to reduce emissions and decouple economic gain from the use of fossil fuels. Emissions have dropped significantly in many developed countries (Aden 2016). Yes, China's emissions are climbing, and it seems to bring another coal-fired power plant online for everyone—one that is decommissioned elsewhere, but real progress is being made.

In many key areas, the technology needed to decarbonize the economy not only exists but is available at scale at a similar cost or cheaper than existing technology. These actions provide proof points for how we can move forward, for there is no doubt we need to move faster (UNFCCC 2020).

OPINION IS CHANGING AND ITS PRO-CLIMATE ACTION

It's hard for humans to understand data and statistics in an actionable manner. We do a substandard job of estimating value, costs, and risks. It's hard for us to plan for the future. It's even more challenging for us to do any of this rationally or consistently over time. Our weak mammalian brains, hard-wired for more prehistoric needs, have a tough time making sense of an incomprehensibly huge existential crisis caused by a bunch of colorless, odorless gasses that have polluted the atmosphere at minute levels, the impacts of which won't be felt for decades or centuries. Behavioral economists like Richard Thaler have studied and documented our individual and collective weaknesses in these areas. We are wired for fight or flight. We tend to react fast to problems that are an immediate, visible threat—but we have a hard time acting on big amorphous issues.

We also hate being told we're stupid. Our collective disrespect for expertise has reached legendary proportions. At times it's downright comical. As the headline in the satirical newspaper, *The Onion*, read on June 16, 1999: "Nation's Experts Give Up." Science and facts have been politicized. Crises like the COVID-19 pandemic only seem to make it worse. Tom Nichols detailed this trend, its causes, and its impacts in *The Death of Expertise* (Nichols 2018).

Somehow despite all of this (and I'm not sure how), we are making progress. Public opinion is changing, and the experts—the scientists, economists, and others—are toiling away undeterred.

As the severity and frequency of these events increases, a widening majority of people in the US see climate change impacting their communities and see it as a significant man-made problem. We feel the impacts more directly, and we are attributing these impacts to climate change. The chart below shows the proportion of adults in the US who say they or their communities are experiencing climate change.

A majority of U.S. adults say climate change affects their local area; 31% say it affects them personally

% U.S. adults who say the effects of global climate change are...

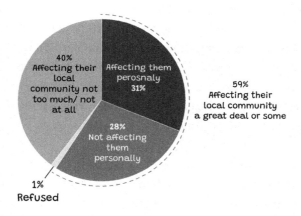

(Hefferon 2019)

Consequently, an increasing proportion of adults in the US believe it should be a high government priority. The chart below shows the rapidly changing public opinion on these issues.

Increased support for prioritizing polices on the environment, climate change since 2011

% U.S. adults who say _____ should be a top priority for the president and Congress

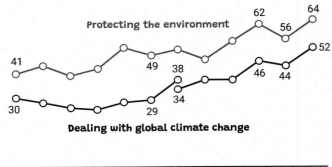

Increasing severe weather has even led to the birth of a new field of study called climate attribution science. Extreme weather events are inherently low-probability, so meteorologists are looking at the likelihood of these individual events under different climate scenarios (Harvey 2018). When heat waves spread across the Pacific Northwest in the summer of 2021 with temperatures exceeding 100 degrees Fahrenheit, climate scientists were able to trace the probability of that extreme event to our shifting climate. We can now see public opinion is turning more definitively.

We are tuning into personal stories. In our discussion, Paula Jasinski, an environmental communications expert, recounted how Chesapeake Bay fishermen are attributing the different fishing patterns. Due to changes in water temperatures and habitat, they are directly seeing the impact of climate change. People internalize and respond best to effects they can see, feel, and connect with personally. We are tuning into these stories more and more. The direct economic costs of severe weather events are being correlated with climate change more readily (Newburger 2021).

In a divided country, it can be hard to find issues where a significant majority have a common understanding of the problem. However, unanimity of opinion around climate change has grown. Protecting the environment and dealing with climate change are top priorities for a majority of American adults, and public support for these priorities has grown significantly and consistently over the last decade or more. Perhaps this is due to us directly experiencing more effects of climate change and making more connections between severe weather patterns and climate change. Over 60 percent of Americans see some local impacts of climate change, and with recent high-profile events, one can anticipate this number will rise. There is also a very significant generational shift in public opinion here. Millennials are significantly more likely to believe climate change is real, human-centered, and will acknowledge we need to take more significant action to address it.

I will add here that, although younger people have stronger feelings about climate change, I think they also feel more helpless to take action. Not everyone feels like they can be the next Greta Thunberg. I have three daughters aged nine to sixteen. As my middle daughter said, "I love what Greta Thunberg is doing, but I have no idea how I could do something like that or if it would even make a difference. It seems like we really need the government and big companies to lead the way." When I discussed this topic with them, this was a common theme, and it was shared by my twenty-year-old goddaughter as well. How do we make it so little actions have consequences, and everyone feels like they can be part of the solution, and everyone feels the impact of their actions?

This feels like the second environmental awakening. It's the same sense of common understanding and purpose that the US and other nations experienced during the ecological movement in the early 1970s that led to titanic shifts in government policy, the passage of the National Environmental Policy Act, The Clean Water Act, The Clean Air Act, the creation of the Environmental Protection Agency, and many other changes in government policy. The current moment seems to be unbowed (and perhaps even reinforced) by the pandemic-induced economic collapse. The following year, or more, may give us the answer with pivotal legislative proposals being debated in the US, a highly anticipated COP26 conference planned for global leaders in late October 2021, the launch of new carbon markets, and other pivotal initiatives.

THE INTERGOVERNMENTAL PANEL ON CLIMATE CHANGE (IPCC)

Perhaps there is no wonkier, drier, stuffier place to find inspiration for how "we can do this" than Geneva, Switzerland, and the World Meteorological Organization. There are no flashy, hard-charging, hyper-organized entrepreneurs and investors here. There are no charismatic politicians espousing visions for the future. It's just the slow, quiet grind of science and policy formation at the global level. It can be maddening. It's lucky Geneva is so damn beautiful. Yet, here—despite our war against expertise—the Intergovernmental Panel on Climate Change (IPCC) toils away and has become the basis for the global consensus around climate change, its causes, and its impacts. Founded in 1988 by the United Nations Environmental Program and the World Meteorological Organization (WMO), the IPCC is the most authoritative voice on the physical science basis of climate change and the impacts and mitigation strategies. It's an odd place to find hope, but indeed I did.

It's remarkable that for more than a generation, nearly thirty-five years, an organization has been able to focus on a single issue and stay at it, undeterred by political pressure or other outside influences. The IPCC was awarded the Nobel Peace Prize in 2007. The reports and the additional information they provide are vital sources of input to international climate change negotiations. It provides the ground truth from which a global consensus can grow. I spoke with Peterri Taalas, the Secretary-General of the WMO, during the lead-up to the publication of the IPCC's Sixth Assessment Report published in July of 2021. Secretary Taalas is from Finland. He's a career scientist, government administrator, and diplomat. He's an *expert*. Peterri is affable and diplomatic. He's patient and makes time for knuckleheads like me. He's serious—but friendly. Funnily enough, he is not made for TV. Most atmospheric scientists aren't. He expresses himself in a staccato Finnish accent that means business.

Through his career, first representing Finland and then broader posts, he's participated in the fact-gathering, synthesis, and consensus-building that is the painstaking work of the IPCC. The Assessment Report compiles the peer-reviewed work of one thousand scientists. Then they gather and curate comments from the 195 member countries, over one hundred thousand comments in all. Despite all of the political pressure, they are able to publish a report that is scientifically solid and nearly uniformly embraced. "The basic principle is everything in the report is based on what is measured or calculated. We have models that are based on the basic laws of physics and the behavior of the system. That's the tool to calculate what's going to happen in the future. They don't go beyond what's in the scientific community" (Taalas 2021). This development is a triumph of expertise over politics and rhetoric.

"The report is very hard to refute. That's why we've seen the political level changes. We have natural variability, but we can also see the impacts of climate change, and they are consistent with the report. The political environment is quite positive." He goes on to expound further on all the positive trends: The European Union has been able to reduce emissions. Emissions are going down in the US. Renewable technologies are affordable and widely available. Many cities and states have ambitious goals.

Nearly 80 percent of the global emissions are under a regime to be carbon neutral by 2050, including the G7 countries. The expectation is that at the next G20 Summit, it will be possible to get the remaining G20 countries to sign on to a net-zero agreement, and the goal is to have 90 percent of the world's emissions covered under the net-zero goal by 2050.

"We are seeing countries and the private sector increasing their commitments." These commitments send a signal to the investment community and the private sector that the demand for new technology will be there. "I'm confident the mitigation changes will happen, but how much warming will there be by the end of this century? That is still the question."

NON-STATE COMMITMENTS

Companies and other non-state actors are taking notice of progress that has been made, and the increasing National Defined Commitments of countries following the Paris Agreement and the most recent IPCC interim report. The Science Based Targets initiative (SBTi) has more than a thousand large companies committing to rigorous goal setting, tracking, and reducing all scopes of its emissions (SBTi). "The Race to Zero" is a United Nations-backed public interest campaign to get non-state actors to sign up to goals that are in line with the Paris Agreement, halving their emissions by 2030 and getting to zero by 2050. Over 2,300 companies, twenty-four regions, seven hundred cities, and one hundred sixty investors have signed on (UNFCCC). "The Climate Pledge," spearheaded by Amazon, Global Optimism, and others, has 106 signatories pledging to reach net-zero by 2040. These initiatives are still in the early stages, and momentum appears to be building.

WE CAN DO THIS

Dr. Taalas's comment perfectly sums up the optimism combined with the uncertainty. We will get there, although we don't know what the destination will look like exactly. There will be more work to do when we get through this transition. We may have messed up some stuff pretty bad by then. It's also possible that this is an incredible opportunity to reshape our built world to be more sustainable, safer, healthier, more resilient, and in closer balance with nature. At the very least, it seems like we still have the means to influence the outcome.

PART 2

PRINCIPLES THAT GET US THERE

"We were meeting companies that were raising the same types of seed rounds of SaaS (software as a service) companies and building products that were cheaper, faster, and better than what they were replacing, and they were chasing trillion-dollar markets. It didn't take us very long to realize actually investing in some of the research technologies might be the fastest way to achieve what we set out to do, which is bring down concentrations of atmospheric CO2."

—CLAY DUMAS, LOWER CARBON

CAPITAL, *TECHSTARS* PODCAST

Climate change is an immensely confounding problem. It's tailored to be cognitively difficult for us to deal with. The impacts of emissions are separated from them by thousands of miles and decades of time. The benefits of action are unclear, far in the future, and shared. The costs of the mitigation efforts are here and now. The action required is collective, not individual. All of these things make acting difficult.

The quote shows what can be done when one takes action. Lower Carbon Capital didn't set out to start a venture fund or to invest in early-stage startups, but they wanted to address the goal of lowering atmospheric CO_2. They took action, iterated, and ended up pursuing a path to achieve that goal.

One of the central premises of this book is that in many ways, and at times deliberately, the climate change math has been made overly complicated. *What would happen if we simplified the climate change problem down to its essential elements and took action?* Would that bias toward action be good? What conditions would help us act? What are the key ingredients of success?

One of the features of the bias toward action is the unintended knock-on consequences that come from it. This idea is embodied in the quote above and the broader approach Lower Carbon Capital has taken. By addressing climate change, they may also disrupt the markets they invest in. Our march toward climate solutions can do a lot to make our economy more efficient and reduce risk. I hope this action also helps us reframe how we view our place in the biome and our relationship within nature as an integral part of it.

These chapters explore our bias toward action, principles of innovation, and how we can better frame the problem to make progress.

CHAPTER 5

The Science of a Bias toward Action

———

"Impossible is not a fact, it's an attitude... There is no way you can deliver victory without optimism."

—CHRISTIANA FIGUERES (TED 2016)

Action is a tricky thing. As humans, we have a bias toward action. It's hardwired into our eager mammalian brains from millions of years of fight or flight. It's also learned and praised throughout our life (Decision Lab). Sometimes that bias toward action isn't a good thing. It leads us to bad investment decisions, unnecessary medical treatments, or riskier situations when staying put would have been the best course of action. There is an excellent study of soccer goalkeeper bias during penalty kicks. Goalkeepers almost always guess and lunge to the left or right. However, the distribution of penalty kicks is around the center of the goal. So the best decision would be inaction, to stay in the center of the goal (Bar-Eli 2007). Humans are also notoriously bad at predicting the future and making decisions to act when necessary. Climate change is a perfect example of this.

Humans are poor at temporal discounting. We overvalue immediate benefits versus longer-term gains. We say we want to invest in the future and create a better world for our children and grandchildren, but in practice, we value the immediate over the long term. We have difficulty understanding cause and effect over long time periods and complex causal relationships (Thaler 2015).

I'm sure, to some degree, the acceleration of action to mitigate climate change is due to our increased ability to tie its effects to present-day consequences of increased droughts, severe weather, wildfires, and other climate-induced effects. Better science has allowed us to make this connection. Extreme weather attribution science is an increasingly established area of climate science. The US National Academy of Sciences published an overview of the field in 2016 (NAS 2016). Despite this advance and countless calls from scientists, economists, and policymakers over decades, we still are just beginning to take action.

What is the cause of our inaction? We worry more about losing something we have than gaining something we don't. We are reluctant to give up any of the things we currently have to get it. Climate change is a big global-scale problem. The cost of taking action falls on the actor, but the benefits will be shared, at least to some extent, globally. We also don't want to take the wrong action. How do we take the right action when the outcome is uncertain? The benefits of action need to be clear and significant—but often, they aren't. So we are hindered by our silly little mammalian brains when it comes to big problems like climate change.

Perhaps the biggest argument for why we delayed action and why action is increasing more rapidly now is our bias toward social norms. We are inclined toward going with the crowd. If everyone is buying gas-guzzling SUVs, we want to as well. Climate change, be damned. However, as we see more and more action being taken, more leaders and popular culture icons leading the way, then we feel more comfortable stepping forward. Teslas have become the coolest thing to drive. Solar panels arrays on house rooftops now seem normal in many areas. Wind farms are becoming passe.

We can see this happening in our own communities. Talking to an old friend, Michael Check, it was funny to hear his observation on this. Michael is a "car guy." His dad was always into them, going to car shows and tinkering with cars. Michael caught the bug. He's also a doctor and a snowboarder, so he moved to Colorado over twenty years ago. He was one of the first and only people in his community to get an electric car, a Nissan Leaf, when they started coming out about ten years ago. "There was maybe only one charging station in the valley," Michael said. "Everyone thought the electric batteries wouldn't make it through the winter or the car wouldn't get through the snow." Anyone who's spent time in Colorado ski towns knows they are four-wheeler territory—large SUVs dominate. Ski towns are also feeling the effects of climate change faster and have a lot to lose. What started out as a novelty or worse has now become mainstream. "I used to have this small group of car guys who were interested in this stuff. When they put in a charging station by the grocery store, I'd go and use it even if I didn't need a charge, just so folks would see it being used and I'd generate some revenue for the company that installed it. Now, it's totally mainstream. There are Teslas everywhere around here."

If climate change is this problem that is perfectly aligned to cause inaction despite our human bias toward action, how do we make progress? Michael's story is a small example of the key. What would happen if we just started doing stuff? Fortunately, we understand a lot of things about taking action.

IT'S PHYSICS

Newton had a lot to say about action. His first law states, "if a body is at rest or moving at a constant speed in a straight line, it will remain at rest or keep moving in a straight line at constant speed unless it is acted upon by a force" (Britannica 2021). If we want to move something, we must put energy into it. We must act. We will stay on our current trajectory—unless we apply force, act, or invest our time, capital, imagination, and other resources into changing it. Every little action counts.

CHANGE IS INCREMENTAL AND INCONSISTENT

We often believe change happens in big leaps. However, progress hides its tracks. Change progresses slowly in small increments, stalls, and plateaus. In his book, Atomic Habits, James Clear talks about breaking big changes down into smaller, more achievable blocks (Clear 2018). Taking action allows this to happen. "Doing small things is easy. Doing big things is hard." James Clear talks about the compounding of one percent improvements over time. Over time, that compounding leads to big improvements happening at an increasing rate. This is similar to the Japanese concept of Kaizen. Incremental change over time results in significant gains. This idea of gradual improvement sounds complicated, and it is. There's even an ancient Marathi word for describing how we start out with lots of enthusiasm and then lose interest—"arambhashura." The steady path of breaking the big climate change problem down into many smaller problems and solutions is what we must do.

At times, this also leads us to threshold conditions that produce more rapid effects. Like the example of ice melting, when those gradual one percent improvements cross a critical threshold. Whether economic, physical, or social—significant changes can happen rapidly. Wind energy and solar power are good examples of this. They are now the fastest-growing energy sources, but that growth only accelerated after they reached cost parity with fossil sources of power.

One way we can do this is by focusing on solutions involving discrete themes based on experience at a local level. For example, Naoko Ishii, the CEO of an investment fund managed by the World Bank called the Global Environmental Facility, has advocated for progress in four specific areas:

- Clean cities
- Zero-carbon energy
- Circular economy
- Food systems

These are broad areas, but immense progress could be made by focusing on just these areas. Progress in these areas would also lead to others (Ishii, 2017).

ACTION CREATES OPPORTUNITY

Another concept of action is it creates new opportunities. Each action leads us to a new end state from which we can journey to the next. With each set of actions, we fill in small pieces of the larger solution set needed. We gather data and gain knowledge that makes the subsequent actions possible. For example, take the development of wind turbines as a renewable zero-carbon source of electricity. They started out small and expensive. Then bigger ones were developed to lower the cost. Then they were connected to the electric grid in better ways to maximize the use of the generated power. Then companies began building them offshore where winds were more constant. Currently, they are beginning to develop them with different shaped fan blades to minimize damage to bird populations and make it easier to deploy wind turbines in more congested settings. Energy storage innovations that enable broader use of intermittent renewable power will likely lead to another step increase in renewable adoption. The initial conditions change after each step. Each innovation builds on the last. Action creates its own opportunity. This concept is described by different people in different ways. Wayne Gretzky is famous for saying, "You miss 100 percent of the shots you don't take." Tom Peters, the renowned business management thinker and writer, said, "Whoever tries to most things wins" (Peters 2016). This was an acknowledgment of the fact that we humans are pretty bad at predicting the

future or calculating odds, but we are really good at trying stuff. We have a bias toward action. For major problems
with uncertain outcomes like climate change, we need to
use that bias.

ACTIONS ARE CONTROLLABLE

One way to fight against all our cognitive limitations is to
realize actions are the only thing we control. We don't control our thoughts or feelings, just our actions. This mentality
is really an eastern concept found in Buddhism and other
modern meditation practices. Our mind has a path of its own.
It just thinks thoughts. That's what it does. We don't have a
lot of control over it. However, we do make decisions about
what actions we take. Actions can also help build momentum
that helps change our thoughts. Action is like a muscle or a
habit. You can train it.

ACTION REQUIRES (AND FOSTERS) OPTIMISM

Action, especially when pertaining to mitigating climate
change, requires optimism. You must believe all the small
changes will add up to a more considerable impact. This
mindset makes sense. What's the point of action if you feel
like no matter what you do, it won't work, or you won't win.
Change can only come with optimism. It doesn't mean you
can't be concerned. Christiana Figueres, former Executive
Secretary of the United Nations Framework Convention on
Climate Change (UNFCCC), has a podcast called *Outrage +
Optimism*. It plays on this concept of being very concerned
and wanting to take immediate action while also being

optimistic. With the initiation of action comes additional benefits: Technology changes. Costs come down. Economic benefits are realized, costs of inaction increase. The actions of a few encourage others to follow. Then it's possible to increase commitments and make them more binding, as we are seeing today.

CHAPTER 6

Principles of Innovation

———

"You know, I love that line, don't waste a crisis."
—MARY POWELL, FORMER CEO OF GREEN

MOUNTAIN POWER (POWELL, 2021)

Never waste a good crisis, as the saying goes. In the case of Green Mountain Power, Mary Powell was the brand new CEO who used the financial problems associated with rate filing (a pricing agreement utilities make with the public utility commissions that regulate them) to reshape the Vermont utility into a clean energy leader. Through crisis, they created a new culture of innovation with a focus on sustainability. Electric utilities are traditionally reliability-driven and asset management-driven cultures where "keep the lights on" is the primary mission. Asset management or management of the rate base (this is the fixed asset costs that the utilities use to calculate the power prices approved by regulators) has traditionally been central to how utilities do business. Innovation and environmental stewardship have not. Green Mountain Power is an example of how utilities and other companies can change their culture to innovate and optimize a broader array of goals with a focus on sustainability. Actions they took in response to a financial crisis helped get them there. Now we'll look at how Innovation is defined on multiple levels and how it's powered by action.

ACTION DEFINES INNOVATION

There are lots of definitions for Innovation. Action is at their core. The Oxford dictionary defines innovation as "the action or process of innovating." Well, that's not very helpful, except for the action part. We have to try some stuff. Part of overcoming the uncertainty associated with climate change is taking action. Action, and the optimism it requires, are also the catalyst of the innovation process we'll explore here at three levels.

Part of the reason for the bias toward action is the principles of innovation and how society adopts new technologies, products, and services in the marketplace. That brings us to another definition: "innovation is the creation, development, and implementation of a new product, process, or service, with the aim of improving efficiency, effectiveness or competitive advantage." This definition puts innovation in the traditional business context. Peter Drucker probably said it best when he said, "Innovation is change that creates a new dimension of performance." But is innovation confined to businesses? I hope not, and I don't think so. We're pretty screwed if that's the case.

President Obama said, "Innovation is the creation of something that improves the way we live our lives" (Hudson 2014). This statement certainly brings us closer to a broad definition that meets the moment. We need regulatory innovation to find new ways to incentivize sustainability. We need market innovation to internalize the societal cost of GHG emissions and streams of ecosystem benefits. We need cultural innovation to change the way we view ourselves and society, not as being apart from nature but rather as being intertwined in it and stewards of it. Note President Obama references "the creation." Action is still the core of his definition. So let me try for a definition that fits the purpose here: *innovation is the action of creating, developing, and implementing institutions, regulations, markets, products, and services that enhance the thriving of all living things.* Okay, shocker, I'm not as eloquent as President Obama or Peter Drucker.

INNOVATION AND SOCIETY

At a societal or sectoral level, innovation trends can be viewed over long stretches of time. John Elkington's book, *Green Swans*, proposes how this process works and will continue to work as we mitigate climate change (Elkington 2020). In his *Green Swan* scenario, the effort to reduce climate change catalyzes the development of various unexpected innovations across many sectors that will produce profoundly beneficial effects. Playing on the book *The Black Swan* by Nassim, Taleb Elkington describes these as "green swans" (Taleb 2007). In action, this is Mary Powell saying, "Never waste a good crisis."

Talib, a polymath who articulates his ideas across a range of mathematics, business, statistics, classics, and history, describes black swans as highly improbable events with three characteristics: 1. They are unpredictable. 2. The events have a massive impact. 3. After the event, we concoct a story to make the event seem less random. From his perspective, the truth is a lot of times that we just don't know, and we are lousy at predicting the future. These are Talib's rare black swans in a flock of white. This idea calls back to Tom Peter's observation that we are bad at picking winners and losers and predicting the future.

Elkington applies these same characteristics to what he believes will come from the necessary innovation we are making to build a more sustainable zero-carbon world. He also describes a process of creation by which he thinks these unpredictably beneficial changes come about. The process entails three "time horizons" in the path toward a future state that he believes will be one of regenerative capitalism. Many innovations need to be developed and scaled along this path. Many of them haven't been invented yet. He draws on examples from the past and how innovations occurred on multiple time horizons to create exponentially better outcomes. In his view, businesses and capitalism are essential drivers of our progress toward sustainability. It's the reworking of the flawed capitalist principles he sees waning today that will lead us to a more sustainable and regenerative form of capitalism in the future. Elkington considers this decade to be a critical inflection point for these trends.

Horizon 1 is "Now," where we find the assumptions supporting current ways of doing business no longer apply or seem outdated. Based on the recent legal cases and stockholder proxy fights with the major oil companies, it appears many are questioning the assumptions underlying their business models. They hold many billions of dollars in assets, as oil and gas reserves. These may be overvalued if the societal cost of utilizing them includes the impacts of climate change.

Horizon 2 is the "Transition." Nascent institutions, regulatory frameworks, technologies, and business models of today are adopted more fully to help mitigate climate change. Think of renewable energy and electric cars. These technologies are ready, but poorly adopted. Carbon-neutral concrete and other technologies are not far behind. To fully adopt some of these technologies, we need changes in regulatory frameworks, infrastructure, and carbon markets.

Horizon 3 is the "Future Steady State." We can't really see this right now. We can see a few components or precursors of this horizon in new ways we work, move, and feed ourselves. We'll need lots of innovation to get there. Perhaps it's cheap hydrogen, structural batteries, small-scale nuclear power production, better ways of growing food, or other technology we can only dream of right now. Perhaps we will have a global agreement on a common carbon market or a better method for verifying carbon sequestration from land and sea conservation. Also, it's hard to see, but do we also need a cultural shift in how we place ourselves in the natural world?

All of this depends on innovation across many institutions and technology development and product adoption at many levels. We'll highlight many examples of this innovation in Part 3. As we discussed in the last chapter, each action and innovation sets the stage and creates the preconditions for the next. For example, artificial intelligence (AI) enabled smart grid technology, better power storage, and more interconnected transmission grids enable greater adoption of distributed renewable energy generation. This is just one example of how all these actions or innovations interconnect and lead to the next.

REGULATORY AND PRODUCT ADOPTION AND THE MARKET

As new products come to market, they go through a product adoption process that has stood the test of time. The figure below provides an overview of this process. What perhaps has changed over time is how these innovations propagate through society. We learn about more things faster thanks to the internet and mobile phones. We rely less on references and word of mouth. Adoption habits also vary by sector. Consumer product adoption curves can be swift. Services like social media and content sharing apps can be adopted virally. Enterprise products or those used by large government agencies and with long usage lives may be adopted more slowly. Not all products and services become mainstream, which is the concept of "crossing the chasm" (Moore 1991).

It's also interesting to note the market players and investors change throughout this process. Both the private sector and public sector play a considerable role. Traditionally, the public sector has driven primary research that leads to early-stage innovation. Today, large private sector and personal investments are being made on new innovations that won't be commercially viable for decades. Commercial space travel is an example of this. Much of the technology development is being funded and led by private companies or personal fortunes for Blue Origin and SpaceX.

Crossing the CHASM

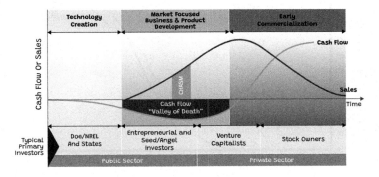

In practice, we see how this plays out for a variety of products and services that are widely adopted below. The particulars vary, but the product adoption curve concept holds up amazingly well. It's interesting to point out that many technologies or products had existed for decades before they were widely adopted. Airplanes were invented in the early twentieth century, but airline travel wasn't widely adopted until the mid-twentieth century. Growing up in the 1970s, getting on a plane was still a pretty big splurge for a middle-class family. At some point, most of these technologies, especially information services, were rapidly adopted once they reached an inflection point (Caroli 2016)

One of the big questions about the changes we need to make to mitigate climate change is will we innovate fast enough? Will we develop, scale, and fully adopt new low- and zero-carbon solutions fast enough to forestall the worst impacts of climate change? As Dr. Taalas said in our interview, "I see the changes being made and commitments to more action. What is still uncertain is what the climate will be like when we reach our emissions goals."

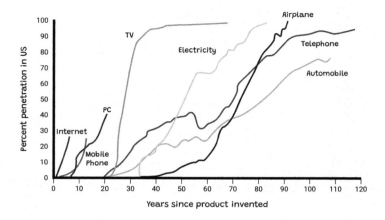

INNOVATION AT THE ORGANIZATION LEVEL

So, how does innovation occur at the organizational or team level? Again, we typically think of innovation as a business process, and the diagram below is indicative of this. But, indeed, governments and regulatory organizations are taking action to find solutions to the challenge of climate change, too. Perhaps the sausage-making process is more chaotic in legislative bodies than it is in corporations, but the general principles still apply.

As the quote from Peter Drucker earlier in this chapter implies, businesses are continuously trying to improve their market position, make their operations more efficient, and develop new products. There is no limitation to the combinations of people, processes, and technology they use to do this. It ranges from systematic to serendipitous. The diagram below is a good summary of how this process works end-to-end within a business.

AN END-TO-END INOVATION PROCESS
Adapting the tools honed by start-ups.

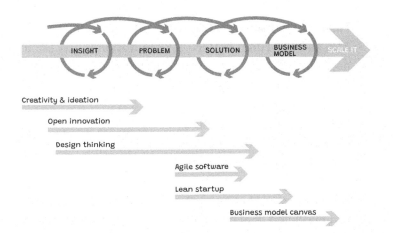

(Furr, 2014)

At the company, institutional, or individual level, a lot of the action and innovation is driven by culture. Like the example of Green Mountain Power at the beginning of the chapter, it boils down to culture. As the saying goes, "culture eats strategy" (Powell 2021). It's fundamentally based on an action bias and optimism. Here are the nine principles of innovation Google uses that exemplify how this is driven forward. What's interesting is none of these are process or organization-driven. They are statements of principle. Yes, they have tons of implications for organization and process, but it doesn't work the other way around (comments to the right of the dash are mine).

Innovation comes from anywhere. We all have something to contribute and a unique perspective (Leong, 2013).

- **Focus on the user**—what does the customer want or need?
- **Aim to be 10 times better**—for innovation to pay off, it needs to be dramatically better than the status quo.
- **Bet on Technical insights**—technical innovation makes new things possible.
- **Ship and integrate**—action!
- **Give employees time**—make innovation a priority.
- **Default to and open process**—share.
- **Fail well**—try hard and learn.
- **Have a mission that matters**—all the definitions of innovation offered above made some value judgment about the outcome. It must have benefits for many.

These principles could fit neatly into many organizations.

WHAT CAN WE TAKE AWAY FROM THE CLIMATE CRISIS?

In many ways, we can apply these same principles for ourselves or our communities in addressing the climate crisis. It's important to remember all these principles are contrived. They aren't laws of nature. Google created them because they believe this leads to the best outcomes for their company and its mission. There are a couple of core attributes worth keeping in mind. Fundamentally, we won't overcome the climate crisis without a lot of innovation across many institutions and sectors at every level.

- **Action**—innovation requires action. We must invest, try, experiment, and implement.

- **Optimism**—no good actions will be taken without hope. We can't think the problem is insurmountable.
- **Iteration**—each innovation sets the preconditions for the next. Don't worry about perfect solutions; look for something good enough for the next step
- **Mission**—the benefits must be for the greater good of society and our biosphere at large.

With the principles of innovation in mind, we can find solutions to the climate crisis at every level.

CHAPTER 7

We Need More Ways to Plug Money into This

———

"We need to create a whole new financial system to support the carbon removal industry."
—JONATHAN GOLDBERG, CEO OF CARBON DIRECT

Reworking our economy and transforming our built world over the next twenty to thirty years will take a massive amount of investment. It's estimated we need approximately $5 trillion per year for the next twenty years to make the transition. The reasons we need all the money go beyond the simple scale of the changes required. Different forms of finance and economic incentives have applications for different segments of the problem and different points on the journey. In this chapter, I discuss some of the reasons why more types of finance are beneficial beyond the simple scale of the problem, and needing every hose available pointed on the fire. Here's an example of how being tied to one financial model can hem us in limiting our ability to address the challenge.

Scott Harris, the founder and CEO of Charity Water, explained during a video conference how he doesn't have the resources to solve the big problem he wants to address. You could argue this is surprising to hear from a very successful nonprofit organization that has installed more than sixty thousand water wells in Africa over the last ten years. "We can't. We have to operate in a completely different way, which slows our growth." He says part of the challenge is the nonprofit mindset that limits his ability to market, pay top salaries, and attract top talent that would allow him to grow. It reminds me of so many aspects of the climate crisis and the resources needed to overcome it. You must put more money into it to reach scale. As Scott said further, "I think it's a billion dollar gift. Yeah, it's a game-changing philanthropic gift that would allow us to then turn a billion into ten." We are going to need a variety of types of capital invested through many types of institutions. Nonprofits can't do it alone. As Scott described further, "I'm constantly faced with old thinking. It's the difficulty of competing or growing or scaling the organization to meet our ambition, just because of the 501c3" (Harris 2021).

As I hope I've made clear in earlier chapters, the climate crisis is huge—dauntingly so. It's understandable to think it's just too hard to solve. As we discussed in Chapters 2 and 3, many problems seem like this at the outset. It's often hard to even develop a plan to move forward. In many cases, a bias toward action is the only way to move forward. Just start doing. The financial component of this challenge is the same. Applying different financing models, experimenting, and iterating will have other benefits as well. We'll discuss those here.

SCALE

One aspect of the dauntingly huge climate challenge is the number of resources it will take. We need to completely retool the built world and the economy—how we produce energy, get around, feed, and shelter ourselves. Given the size of the investment, the outcome is uncertain. As discussed in the last chapter, we can't see all the innovations over the horizon. We know we need a lot more money. Fortunately, this isn't a one-dimensional challenge. There are many components to the overall solution, and all of them will be used in concert. There are many financing challenges to address.

The scale of the change required is part of what drives the staggering need for investment. The fossil fuel-based energy sector alone is enormous. A study by Morgan Stanley looked at the investment needed in five energy- and transportation-related areas—renewables, electric vehicles, carbon capture and storage, hydrogen, and biofuels—and an estimated $50 trillion was needed in these areas combined (Klebnikov 2019). Other sectors and solutions will cost more.

Government funding of conservation programs and non-profit environmental program budgets are dwarfed by fossil industry subsidies. In his role as staff director of the Agriculture Committee in the US Senate, Chris Adamo noted how the myriad of other government programs could all be turned to help provide support for climate change mitigation programs. The full variety of financial solutions helps meet the scale challenge.

These numbers seem daunting, but within the scale of the over $90 trillion GDP per year global economy (World Bank), $5 trillion for twenty years doesn't sound so daunting. It's also important to remember we get cool stuff for that $100 trillion—cleaner air and water, less social unrest, more nature, longer lifespans, and more whales. We will have to accept fewer Cadillac Escalades.

In fact, anything powered by fossil fuels, just start chucking it now. This brings us to the next benefit of more financial resources: time.

TIME

Time is another element of the problem. In his book The Case for Climate Capitalism, Tom Rand points out that when we need to solve the problem fast, we care less about efficiency and more about the rate at which we can generate change. He describes this as the leaky hose. "If your house is burning down, you care less about the efficiency of the delivery of the water than about the sheer volume of water" (Rand 2020). A big, leaky hose is better than a precise drip irrigation system that would deliver a precise amount of water very efficiently. It's worth pointing out what this implies: the more time we let slip away, the more investment we will need and the less efficient it will be. The ride could get bumpy. We'll also end up needing more investment for adaptation as we let the problem slip further into the future. The solutions get more costly and inefficient as we delay. Imagine a world with strict moratoriums or rationing of certain types of activities. The cost and disruption of these types of remedies are high.

This is where the private sector acting at scale in the ecosystem services arena could have a sizable impact. As Tim Male pointed out, "the US spent $2.7 trillion on the 5G rollout to upgrade cellular communications. It happened fast with a minimum of regulatory hurdles. In conservation, we spend so much time trying to get buy-in. We need to act much faster." If you are a resource-driven company— which means just about any company providing food, fiber, or raw materials—the scope of the emissions in your supply chain is driven by ecosystem services. Acting to decarbonize that through conservation investment could move lots of money fast without the need for lengthy approval processes. Investing more through multiple streams of capital now also builds buy-in and support.

TRUST—BUY-IN

Building a broader constituency and trust is another reason for expanding financial avenues to solve the problem. This reminds me of a problem from my own work. Over the years, it's been immensely hard to build and sustain sufficient surface weather observing networks, especially in the developing world, to support the needs of global weather prediction models. There is immense value in this information for resiliency and supporting day-to-day commercial activity. Traditional government and donor-funded project finance fall short. Programs are episodic, poorly managed, and few constituents are brought into the fold to support infrastructure that has a broad potential use. Creating a public-private partnership model brings more potential funding sources into the fold and more stakeholders invested in (and in some ways dependent upon) its success. This encourages companies to take more risks and invest their own capital in deploying and managing the networks. They then create a commercial market of the network services that can finance additional development and support. With the proper buy-in from multiple stakeholders, the network becomes self-sustaining and compounding.

DIFFERENT PROBLEMS NEED DIFFERENT MONEY

As Jonathan Goldberg stated in our interview, "The financing infrastructure needed to address just one part of the challenge is":

- We need financial measures and incentives to encourage large public companies to consider the climate risks on their balance sheets and, ultimately, their income statements.
- We need infrastructure spending that considers the climate cost of CO_2 emissions.
- We need financial models and regulatory structures that internalize and provide incentives for the stacked ecosystem services associated with better management and preservation of diverse ecosystems on land and in the oceans.

All these financial tools and structures are needed at scale. If we are successful, people will make a lot of money reducing CO_2 levels by emitting less and removing and sequestering more. Reducing, removing, and sequestering CO_2 and other GHGs should be profitable.

Add to this the need for many other types of financing to support other parts of the problem:

- Grant funding for basic research
- Venture funding to launch startups
- Private equity to further scale and commercialize
- Government incentives, impact bonds, conservation banks, and other types of investment vehicles to support conservation and green infrastructure spending.

The list goes on.

EXTERNALITIES AND ECONOMIC INCENTIVES

Internalizing all the economic benefits is another reason for utilizing a wide variety of financial structures. Tim Male does a wonderful job of describing this aspect in the instance of the Chesapeake Bay conservation efforts. A broad array of private capital combined with government tax incentives and more traditional conservation programs brings together a variety of different incentives that fit different types of programs to improve the health of the Chesapeake Bay. Tax policies reward investment in open space. Pay for Success contracting improves wetlands restoration. Water funds pay farmers who improve cropping practices that improve water quality for municipalities. Virginia has set up forest banks that offset ecosystem services lost through development efforts. Each of these is a different type of financial vehicle fitted to the needs of different kinds of programs to improve the health of the Chesapeake Bay. All of them internalize the ecosystem benefits in different ways. They are fit for purpose and the context of the local situation. In Chapter 12, I will look more deeply into some of the financial models being developed and the stories of the people on the front lines.

RECAP

Mitigating climate change and responding to its impacts will require all these types of programs. We just need a lot more money. We need more money because of the sheer scale. It's a *huge* problem. We need more money because of its complexity. It involves nearly every aspect of our economy and the built world. We need more types of money because of the limited time we have to respond. We must make big changes fast, and efficiency is not the number one thing we are solving for; it's speed and impact. We need more money because we need to build broader coalitions of support for the required changes. Everybody needs to be bought in. Finally, we need new and diverse financial tools to support climate adaptation and mitigation initiatives. Many of these are at the local level, but we need to standardize and scale them for broader adoption.

CHAPTER 8

Regulation Plays a Big Role

"It's not an either-or, for me it's a YES."
—CHRIS ADAMO, WHEN ASKED IF WE NEEDED
MORE INVESTMENT FINANCING, MARKET-
BASED SOLUTIONS, OR REGULATIONS.

It's common for the prescriptions for solutions to climate change to exhibit a healthy dose of simplistic black and white thinking. Either capitalism is the entire problem, and we must upend our social-political order, or purely voluntary market-based solutions are the savior. Often, these solutions seek to assign blame. We need a more pragmatic and opportunistic approach.

One common thread throughout this book is that *diversity is good*. Complexity is good. In the natural world, healthy ecosystems are diverse and complex (it's also true, healthy ecosystems sequester more carbon). As we saw in the last chapter and will discuss further in Chapter 12, the financial system to funnel resources to climate change initiatives entails a complex web of grant funding, venture capital, project finance, credit, catalytic capital, public markets, rating agencies, insurers, and other institutions. We need a wide array of green, blue, black, and gold carbon solutions to decarbonize human activity (see Part 3). We also need a complex network of government regulations to nudge our society forward and create the necessary incentive structures.

Part of the reason why the US continued to make modest progress on climate change during the preceding years of resistance and backsliding at the federal level was the commitments and progress made by cities and states. Regional GHG cap-and-trade schemes continued to grow. With their myriad of policy and regulatory initiatives, many jurisdictions made new commitments and progress. The UNFCCC "Race to Zero" initiative claims 733 cities and 31 regions as members that have made net-zero commitments (UNFCCC). Cities have a lot of power here. Most people live in cities. Cities run bus fleets, electric utilities, water authorities, and have massive spending power. It's often perceived that complex regulatory frameworks are inefficient and bureaucratic. Certainly, they can be. They can also better account for local economic conditions, regulatory frameworks, and customs. Modern information technology makes the complexity more manageable.

Policy and regulatory frameworks also help de-risk investments by the private sector and create the financial incentives for progress. Here we explore further wisdom behind a blended, complex regulatory-based, and market-based approach.

BIDEN FLOODS THE ZONE

It's early March 2021 when I get a chance to reconnect with Eric Waeckerin. We first met when he was a newly minted environmental lawyer in Washington, DC. The Biden administration has recently barnstormed into town, implementing an unprecedented wave of far-reaching executive orders and policy initiatives related to climate change.

Eric looks the same as the first time I met him over twenty years ago. It's 4:00 p.m. on a Thursday, and he's wearing a baseball cap with mountains and fish on it. He's every bit a man of the mountain west. He's friendly, easy-going, and speaks with the relaxing pace common to a rancher or a ski bum. Eric's countenance does not give away that he's a skilled lawyer, a partner at a top Denver firm, and helping big corporations—mainly oil and gas companies—navigate the Clean Air Act and associated state regulations. From where he sits, you see how all-encompassing and challenging the migration to a zero-carbon economy is.

Eric has been an environmental lawyer for more than two decades, working on a variety of issues. He grew up in Wyoming and got into environmental policy because of his college professor Jason Shogren. Jason is this amazing guy who lives out in Centennial, forty miles west of Laramie. He won a Nobel Prize for his ground-breaking work on environmental economics. He's done a ton of fantastic research, he's a huge Dylan fan, and he has his own band. Eric gets excited as he's telling me this. "He really inspired me. You know, growing up in Wyoming, it's a hyper-conservative political environment. It's a very unique place to grow up and then be involved in environmental policy for my career." For most of his career, environmental issues moved at a slow pace. Now he sees decades of movement in months, but there are so many hurdles to cross and questions left unanswered.

"This has been a crazy three months since Biden took over. That executive order, you know, you could tell they'd been working on it for a long time. I'm sure a lot of the more prominent NGOs (non-government organizations) contributed to it. That framework, you don't just roll out an executive order that long and sweeping on the first day without a ton of preparation. It's a broad government sweep. It has almost nothing to do with the EPA. It's injecting climate change into every part of the federal government."

Sure enough, Eric is right. A group of more than one hundred fifty policy experts with extensive government expertise worked on the Climate 21 Project in advance of the Biden Administration taking office to develop a set of recommended initiatives that could be implemented with existing regulatory authority (The Climate 21 Project 2021). The idea was to hit the ground running. The recommendations encompass eleven White House offices, federal departments, and agencies. It calls to "mobilize a whole-of-government climate response." Here, the aim is not a policy agenda but more of a nuts-and-bolts administrative agenda to inoculate climate change into every relevant government decision or action. It makes climate change a priority for leaders at every level of the federal government. It recommends working the 2021 fiscal year budget and beyond to prioritize climate initiatives. It calls for quickly reallocating staff to climate positions left vacant or reclassified by previous administrations. There are hundreds of recommendations across all the departments and agencies. All of them are intended to be implemented within the first one hundred days of the administration. This is an example of the surprisingly diverse and expansive set of tools the government has to address a given issue.

LIMITATIONS OF MARKETS

As someone who's received a lot of economics training, I hate to admit it, but markets have limits, especially voluntary ones. If we want to limit CO_2 emissions, why can't we just put a price on them? If we want to make the reduction of emissions as cost-efficient as possible, why can't we just make the right to emit tradeable, so market participants who can reduce emissions at the lowest cost per unit do it the most?

There are some great examples where emissions trading schemes have worked very well. Although, none that I'm aware of have been voluntary. Regulatory frameworks are at the center of every established market of any scale I can think of. Even markets we think of as being free and open are constructed with significant guardrails and guidelines to ensure transparency, liquidity, and to avoid fraud and abuse. There are wonderful examples of what happens when we don't have adequate market definition and regulation: remember Enron of 2003 or the mortgage loan crisis of 2008–2009?

The emissions trading market for sulfur dioxide (SO_2) and nitrous oxide (NOX) is probably the most successful and long-running emissions trading market in the US—and possibly the world. It was established in the 1980s. If you're old enough, you might remember acid rain. Heavy manufacturing and coal-powered electric generation facilities in the rust belt spewed SO_2 and NOX into the atmosphere, creating acid rain that killed forests in the northeast US and polluted rivers and streams. The markets successfully reduced the amount of these pollutants. A cap-and-trade scheme was created that limited the number of emissions each polluter could emit. Emitters could trade their permits so the most cost-effective sources of emissions reductions could be maximized. Emitters adapted, changed their processes, and adopted new technology to reduce emissions. Over time, the total amount of emissions permits were ratcheted down. Sounds simple; why won't this work for CO_2 and methane? The answer is, it will—and it won't be enough

SO_2 and NOX emissions had some unique properties that made it easier to regulate them via a cap-and-trade system. These are point source pollutants, meaning the emissions came from specific operations that generated these pollutants. It all came out of smokestacks. The emissions could be easily quantified. The impacts were localized—regional, not global. Finally, the pollutants decompose faster in the environment. We aren't so lucky with CO_2. The sources and sinks are as complex and varied as the global carbon cycle we discussed in Chapters 2 and 3. It's not just a pollutant. It's an essential part of life, and the primary way carbon finds its way into living things. Indirectly, that includes humans. This doesn't mean we can't use markets to help reduce some sources of

CO2. In fact, we do, and those markets are expanding. China has launched its market, and all other markets in the world are growing. However, we need a much larger tool set to address all the CO2 emissions that need to be reduced.

Different sectors may need different sets of solutions to work. Cap-and-trade schemes have been shown to work well for large point source emitters—factories, power plants, etc.—but the land sector is different, as are other industries. Not only is the physical problem different, but the people involved, their beliefs, and the associated policies and political preferences are different. It's hard to fully characterize, but these practical realities of humans all trying to work together to solve a problem with our lizard brains make the optimal set of solutions (not necessarily the most elegant, theoretically efficient) vary dramatically. In summary, a market-based cap-and-trade system is often touted as a comprehensive solution, but it has its limitations.

Eric made this point to me about the experience in Colorado. There was a cap-and-trade proposal The Environmental Defense Fund (EDF) put forward that ultimately got rejected. "The proposal EDF was pushing was really interesting. It allocated allowances that could be traded through auctions and the allowances would be ratcheted down over time. Like the California market." The ultimate conclusion was it was too complicated and not politically viable in a state that has a significant amount of heavy industry and oil and gas. It also wasn't clear if the scheme would work in a medium-sized state. The market could function more efficiently at the regional or national level with enough market participants to create liquidity and lower transaction costs. Ultimately, Colorado passed a bill creating emissions targets and is developing a command and control road map to regulate industries to lower emissions levels. But that isn't a simple path, either (Waeckerlin 2021).

POLITICAL REALITIES

Chris Adamo, vice president of government affairs for Danone, is a ball of energy and optimism. He'd already been up and working for an hour when we started our 7:30 a.m. video call. He was chowing down an egg sandwich, which he said his wife had just passed him. Chris provides great insight into the vagaries and practicalities of the political decision-making process that creates policy. In this arena, the most elegant solution, in theory, gives way to what is possible. Different constituents layer on all kinds of value judgments into the process, "and I think that's really important because you get into some ideologies here, where people are arguing for just privatization or just government regulation and that dogma I'm not into that. I'm not in that dogma fight. I'm not here to prove an ideology" (Adamo 2021).

The policy-making process, from lawmaking to promulgating regulations, to budgeting and staffing at federal, state, and local levels, all gets politicized. There are opportunities to make progress, big and small, throughout. It's just the reality of the system we operate in, and I don't think it's any different in Beijing than it is in Washington, Brazil, Brussels, Austin, Albany, or Sacramento. Ultimately, this reflects the varied attitudes we all have about this all-encompassing issue. Again, we need diverse solutions to meet local conditions.

As Eric points out, all of this sits on top of a public that is divided in many respects (see Chapter 4). Certainly, climate issues are being talked about a lot. "For most of my career, environmental issues progressed at a slow pace. These weren't issues that captured a lot of national attention, but I was sitting down with my father-in-law the other night, and we were talking about climate change, energy policy, nuclear power, and Bill Gates's new book. Those kinds of conversations never used to happen." I asked Eric if public opinion is changing, and he starts by saying "Yes," but adds, "Well, it's because of all the folks from California moving to the Rockies." As I write this while my plane in Houston boards for Denver, a man walks down the aisle in front of me wearing a t-shirt that reads "Don't California My Wyoming."

NEED FOR ALL THE TOOLS

As we know, it's going to take a lot of resources to retool society to get to zero emissions. We then will need an equally broad reworking of all our incentive structures—regulations, rules, grant programs, technical support, oversight, and the rest—that the government provides to get where we need to go. In part, this is where the Biden administration's whole-of-government approach makes sense. As Chris described the problem, "You look at all the philanthropic base and all the government budgets across the world, those budgets and that revenue stream doesn't meet the problem [...] If I just go work for a regular environmental group or if I just advocate for existing policy initiatives, that isn't bad, but the baseline isn't changing. We need to change the baseline. We need new creative ideas to get at the problem."

In some ways, the political economy of this ensures the easy stuff will get done first. Government action also catalyzes private sector action. Even nonbinding or more general commitments at the global level, like the National Defined Contributions (NDC's), dictated in the UNFCCC Paris Climate Accords, send signals and help de-risk private sector investment.

As the World Resources Institute report on the policy framework to decarbonize put it, "Given the magnitude of the decarbonization challenge, there is no doubt more action will be required by all levels of government in the United States" (Bianco 2020).

NEED FOR SOLUTIONS AT ALL LEVELS AND ALL SECTORS

Significant global policy wins like the Paris Climate Accords get a lot of news, but it can be hard to see how they create real change. Their influence is less direct, but talk to the leader of any public company that's a large emitter, and they will tell you it matters (Chapter 12). They are reacting to changes at that level. Federal rules have a more considerable influence, and it goes well beyond purely regulatory power. The federal government spends a ton of money. It has market influence. If we decided all US postal service vehicles had to be electric vehicles by a specific date, it's safe to say that would drive spur a lot of supply of these vehicles for other purposes. The federal laws also provide a lot of technical expertise, grant funding, and other incentives. Whether it's via extension services for farmers, conservation tax credits for land owners, or other programs, they all have immense influence. Federal rules also set a baseline—a required minimum standard—for state regulations in many cases.

State and local governments, in many ways, are the location of much of the important action. "States and local governments are more knowledgeable about their local circumstances, enabling them to develop solutions that fit their unique context and are responsive to local equity issues. State and local governments have been acting for years in areas that are within their primary jurisdiction, including the regulation of electric utilities, building codes, land-use planning, zoning, agriculture, waste management, and more. As a result, states and localities have accumulated invaluable experience and expertise, which will be critical for the success of future federal climate programs" (Hultman 2021).

If there is a problem with this complexity, it's that it takes time, and we don't have a lot. There is an immensely complex and slow process of moving policy forward at the state and local levels. For years, mostly during the Trump administration, while federal policy lagged, state and local actors, along with the private sector, continued to make significant progress on climate change. As Joseph Kane of the Brookings Institute said, "The Trump decision [to leave the Paris Agreement] was a setback for us all in dealing with climate change...the US and the global community continued to move forward... Domestically, in the US, we saw a tremendous groundswell of sub-national action with different states, cities, business ... Action continued forward." But this progress isn't easy. "In Colorado, we've been working on climate change regulations ever since I moved here ten years ago." The change in tone at the federal level has accelerated this discussion. Climate change was a significant issue during the 2020 presidential campaign, and that has added urgency. A lot more needs to be done at the local level to decarbonize. There are a ton of problems that need to be worked through (Kane 2021).

The table below is an excellent example of this complexity in Colorado. There are different solutions for every sector.

Table 1: Emissions Reduction Estimates by Sector, Action, and Timeline (MMT Co2e)

Emissions Sector	Action	2025 Reduction	2030 Reduction	Regulatory Actions	Legislative Action	Timeline
Recent, Ongoing, and Near-Term Actions						
Electric Power	Electric Generation Sector Transition	18.90	32.20	Adopt Regional Haze Limits; AQCC Clean Energy Plan Guidance	None	Regional Haze Rulemaking Hearing: November 19 & 20, 2020 (Reg 3 and 23)
Oil and Natural Gas	Ongoing SB181 Rulemaking (Reg 7)	7.00	12.00	AQCC Rulemaking (Reg 7); COGCC Rulemaking	None	Ongoing (Dec 2019, Sept 2020). Comprehensive rulemaking scheduled for December 16 & 17, 2021
Coal Mining and Abandoned Mines	Coal Mine Methane Rulenaking	5.00	6.00	AQCC Regional Haze Rulemaking (Reg 3 and 23); APCD Permits	None	Regional Haze Rulemaking Hearing: November 19 & 20, 2020 Ongoing (for permits)
Transportation	Business as Usual: CAFE AND LEV[1]	5.00	6.00	No action required	None	n/a
Transportation	Comprehensive Efforts[2]	2.00	4.60	AQCC 2021-2023 Rulemaking	Potential Legislative Authorization and Appropriations	Initial Rulemaking scheduled for July 2021

Emissions Sector	Action	2025 Reduction	2030 Reduction	Regulatory Actions	Legislative Action	Timeline
Transportation	ZEV Regulations and Utility Transportation Electrification Plan	0.40	1.50	1. Adopt ZEV Standard 2. Engage with PUC re: Utility Transportation Electrification Plan Approvals	None	1. Complete: ZEV Standard adopted August 2019 (Reg 20) 2. Ongoing
Industrial Processes	HFC Phase Out	0.56	1.15	Adopt HFC Phase Out Rules	None	Complete: HFC Phase Out Rules adopted May 2020 (Reg 22)
Waste Management	Front Range Waste Diversion Enterprise Implementation	0.50	0.50	No action required.	None	Complete
Multiple	Local Action Programs	1.00	2.50	No action required.	None	n/a
Total Emissions Reductions (MMT CO2e):		40.36	66.45			
Emissions Reductions Needed to Meet Goals (MMT CO2e)[3]:		35.07	67.45			

(Van Winkle, 2020)

Eric talked about a few examples that illustrated the complications at the local level. For example, various industrial operations use large diesel motors—huge ones, over a thousand horsepower. They are used in remote oil and gas operations as backup generators for data centers and other applications. They emit a lot of NOX. "The silver bullet solution would be to replace them with electric motors," but then you need reliable power at all of these locations. The rule was expected to take effect in one year, but these engines last for twenty or thirty years. The utilities have thirty-year planning horizons for grid investments. It's hard to figure out how we are going to get broad electrification of this sector. "I think it's so complex it's almost hard to comprehend," Eric stated. At a macro level, we've invested billions, yet only 3 percent of our energy supply comes from renewables. It's a decidedly tricky problem to solve.

Carbon capture and storage is widely promoted as a possible solution, especially by oil and gas companies and other large-scale emitters that have significant challenges in decarbonizing their business models. But it hasn't really been done. Is it safe? Where can it be done? Oil and gas companies certainly hope to make it a big part of their value chain going forward, but there isn't a federal permit class for sequestration operations. It gets delegated to the states to promulgate regulations. It takes years to do this, and only a couple of states have managed to do it so far. The complications are complex and real.

In many ways, Eric's perspective embodies the practical challenges ahead. Often creating the technical solutions, "the Miracle"—as John Elkington describes technological advancements in *Green Swans*—is the easy part. Implementing them broadly in a complex world and building support for them takes longer, and there's no simple technological hack for a skeptical public. Private sector providers of zero- or negative-carbon solutions would benefit significantly from clear and consistent support and legal and regulatory direction. How can Washington move faster to provide it? We can't forget about the importance of government policy of all varieties at all levels.

PART 3

EXISTENCE THEOREMS

"We are continually faced with a series of great opportunities brilliantly disguised as insoluble problems."

—JOHN W. GARDNER

A few years ago, I participated in a panel discussion at the World Bank on public-private partnerships in the meteorological sector. There is no precedent for them in the sector, and there is lots of skepticism on whether they can work. Few could see how a commercial relationship between a government agency and the private sector could be approved by World Bank bureaucracy or be culturally accepted in host countries.

Berrien Moore, dean of the College of Atmospheric Sciences and Geography at the University of Oklahoma, was on the panel. I've been professionally acquainted with him for several years, and he is a highly respected lion of the field. He said, "What we need here are *existence theorems!*" We need to show that it can be done. We need to demonstrate that what seems impossible or impractical is better—cheaper, more accessible, faster, and producing better outcomes. Addressing the climate challenge is no different than the problem we faced in this obscure workshop on public-private partnerships.

Everything seems impossible until it's not. The climate challenge is too big and intractable—until we (humans) *invent* the solutions. We can't foresee how we will create the many thousands or millions of new technologies, applications, policies, financial models, ways of collecting and communicating data, and so on that are required to transform our economy, our built world, and how they fit within the natural world.

Invention is magic. Making something possible that was impossible before, creating something that didn't exist—that's magic. According to the Oxford Dictionary, the word "magic" is defined as "the power of apparently influencing the course of events by using mysterious or supernatural forces." The act of invention is making the mysterious and supernatural seem ordinary. As Arthur C. Clarke said, "The only way to discover the limits of the possible is to go beyond them into the impossible."

The optimism I hope comes through in this book is born out of the stories of the people in the chapters that follow. There are so many brilliant, hardworking, well-intentioned, and wonderful people who are working on the thousands and millions of magic acts necessary to address climate change. They are trying to create those existence theorems through acts of invention that make the impossible possible—like magic. Again, it's action and innovation that define these acts of creation. I can honestly say that I think we can do this. We got this! And, of course, we must.

CHAPTER 9

Green Carbon

"Nature doesn't only need us to save it. Humanity needs nature if we hope to survive."

—SARAH KAPLAN (KAPLAN, 2021)

The opening quote calls back to the Introduction. Over the long term (think geologic or ecological scales of time, not human scales), nature will be fine. It doesn't need us to save it. Humans undoubtedly gain a great deal from nature. It supplies the air, water, and nutrients we need to fuel our existence. It provides the material for our shelter and energy for our production. It processes our waste, transforming it from harmful to useful. Let's not forget to mention we reap a great deal of comfort and psychological benefit knowing that intact, pristine ecosystems exist and thrive at scale. These are the stacked ecosystem benefits we reap for "free,"—meaning outside of how our economy values the system. Nature certainly DOES need us if we want to sustain what we think of as healthy, intact ecosystems. This chapter is about these benefits that flow from our land. It's about how we value these benefits and how we enhance them to help us overcome the climate challenge.

When most people think of food, they think of their favorite restaurant, their favorite meal, or maybe the grocery store. If you're my youngest daughter, you just think of ice cream, and that's it. For the most part, we are divorced from the long and complex web that supplies food to our table. Even more so, when we think of our homes, the paper we write on, and the stuff we use to wipe our rear ends, we have a vague thought about the material used to make them, how it's grown, harvested, processed, and disposed of. Yet to tackle climate change, the land sector—our farms, forests, and wetlands—are going to play a considerable role.

SETTING THE STAGE—THE LAND SECTOR CHALLENGE

Agriculture and forestry are currently significant emitters of GHGs. They could also be part of the web of nature-based solutions to remove substantial amounts of CO_2 from the atmosphere and sequester it as organic carbon in our soils and forest biomass. But like many natural systems, it's complicated. The biology and chemistry are hard to understand, harder to model, and truly difficult to nail down to the numerical specificity needed to commoditize carbon sequestration credits. You have millions of land owners in the US and billions of people who work the land worldwide. Getting them to adopt new management techniques through a myriad of incentives and regulations isn't easy. How do we tackle the problem?

Globally about 24 percent of GHGs come from agriculture. Some of this total is from clearing forests to make more room for cattle grazing, palm oil plantations, and farming. In the US, due in part to more modern agricultural practices and a more robust industrial and consumer sector, agriculture only contributes about 10 percent of GHG emissions (Popkin 2020). However, it can also serve as an effective sink to sequester as much as 10 percent of all GHG emissions by some estimates.

Like a lot of the things we do to support human life, agriculture has a carbon footprint. Breaking the topsoil and exposing it to the air releases CO_2. This is not inherently a bad thing. It provides us with the food and fiber we need. However, "recent estimates suggest that some 133 billion tons of carbon, roughly a fourth of all carbon emitted by humans since the Industrial Revolution, has been lost from soils globally" (Popkin 2020). Methane is the second most important GHG, with nearly a fifth of the climate change impact, and the largest source of methane is agriculture (UNFCCC 2021). Could we adopt better agronomic and land management practices to put that soil carbon back in the ground?

Modern farming practices and technological advances that have resulted in vast improvements in farm productivity have come at a cost to the climate. Farm machinery, chemicals, and fertilizer rely on fossil fuels. Excessive amounts of fertilizer added to soils can cause microbes to emit N_2O, another potent greenhouse gas. In some ways, this feels analogous to the challenge faced in marine ecosystems. In search of more production—higher yields, in this case, larger catches in the marine example—we've depleted the stock. Now we must keep putting more inputs, water, fertilizer, and pesticides into the soil to achieve high production yields. Could regenerative agriculture help reverse this trend?

Modern forestry and wetlands management pose a huge problem and potential promise as well. Today, many of the world's forests are stripped for their lumber and then cleared for agriculture and ranching. Wetlands are degraded for development or filled to make way for agricultural land. Protecting them, restoring them, and sustainably managing them promises to turn forests and wetlands from a source of GHGs to a net sink.

THE RISE OF REGENERATIVE AGRICULTURE

The hope is newer agronomic techniques, broadly termed "regenerative agriculture" (also called climate-smart agriculture), can bring carbon to rest in soils stripped of their organic matter for generations. This, in turn, will improve soil health, helping to maintain yields while reducing the reliance on irrigation, chemicals, and fertilizer. The kicker is these farming techniques will create a stream of ecosystem benefits, such as improved water quality, reduced erosion, and better flood protection, which will generate additional income streams for farmers.

Regenerative agriculture consists of a myriad of farming practices, many of which are not new, that vary depending on the region, the crops being produced, the size of the farm, and other factors. These techniques upend many of today's dominant farm practices. Generally speaking, they entail growing more types of crops within a detailed crop rotation system and, in many cases, bringing crop and animal production closer together to occupy the same land. For generations, agricultural practices have been trending in the opposite direction. Large-scale monoculture production has been favored for its efficiency and precision. Animal production has been increasingly segregated from crops and moved indoors.

The stakes are high. Agriculture has the opportunity to be a source or a sink of CO_2 in the global climate fight. "'This makes soil both a ticking time bomb and an overlooked climate solution,' said Asmeret Asefaw Berhe, a soil biogeochemist at the University of California at Merced. Better soil stewardship could reduce emissions by at least 5.5 gigatons of carbon dioxide each year—about 15 percent of current annual emissions" (Kaplan 2021). The effects of climate change could also drive the release of more CO_2 from the land sector. Warming temperatures could cause more crop failures due to pest infestations, droughts, and floods. Other feedback loops could also worsen methane emissions as well.

Nitrous oxide (N_2O) is also a significant concern. Poor nutrient management and the interaction of synthetic fertilizer with soil moisture and other factors can lead to a spike in N_2O emissions. This is another area where impressive innovation is taking place. Pivot Bio has invented a bio-tech solution that can replace much of the synthetic fertilizer. Pivot Bio is one of many sustainable agriculture tech companies raising eye-pooping sums of venture funding (Feldman 2021).

I say "the hope" in the first sentence of this section partly because there are so many unknown factors about how some of these trends will play out on a global scale. Commodities markets are global. If regenerative agriculture practices reduce yields in the US, does that cause more of the Amazon rainforest to be cleared so we can put more land under the plow there to meet global demand? What if the demand for ethanol as a biofuel increases and further crowds out land for food production? It's an extensive and dynamic global system.

As the Biden administration has settled in and cabinet posts and other key positions are filled, you can get a sense of the centrality of climate change policy. The land sector is an integral part of this calculus. Even though agriculture and forestry may represent a smaller component of the climate challenge than transportation, energy, and materials production, there are some unique aspects of the policy environment where rapid change could occur. No one is more important to delivering that change than returning Secretary of Agriculture Tom Vilsack.

The Biden administration and entrepreneurs are pulling out all the stops, implementing many programs, and experimenting with numerous business models to promote regenerative agriculture as a means to fight climate change, improve environmental benefits, and improve farm incomes. "Vilsack made clear that he shares President Biden's vision of net-zero agriculture, but the efforts farmers are already undertaking—cover cropping, focusing on soil health—need to be incentivized with market opportunities" (Reiley 2021). One recent step taken is the rollout of a climate partnership initiative to create revenue opportunities for producers using climate-smart practices (USDA 2021).

Secretary Vilsack is an unassuming guy with an amazing career in public service. In the era of personal brand politics, Tom is a throwback to a time of the "true believer" in Washington—the non-ideological person who comes to Washington to work on issues, who believes in debate and compromise. This is the type of person who truly wants to make things better through sound policy and believes the government has a role in making people's lives better.

His personal story, though told many times, is worth recounting. In interviews, he sounds like a football coach at a press conference, dispassionately reviewing his performance. Whether it's western Pennsylvania or Iowa, it's all Midwest. He personifies that broad American idiom. He was born in Pittsburgh and adopted from a Catholic orphanage. His adoptive home, though loving, had its hardships as well. There were economic challenges, and his mother suffered from substance abuse. He says growing up in this environment teaches you to be a pleaser and a problem solver—those traits and his desire to serve come through.

What he has that the Biden administration perhaps values most for implementing its climate policy is a track record for getting things done, a deep knowledge of the many billions of dollars in funding the US Department of Agriculture (USDA) distributes each year, and loyalty. For the land sector, the USDA is the train much of the Biden administration's climate policy ambitions run on, and Secretary Vilsack is the engineer. He is tasked with orienting about $56B in federal farm subsidies, farm credit, conservation programs, rural economic development, electrification, and other spending toward addressing climate change in the land sector. It's this policy framework that makes the land sector such a rich target for progress within Biden's "whole government" plan to combat climate change.

Secretary Vilsack comes from a farming community. As returning Secretary of Agriculture and former governor of Iowa, he understands farmers. He's trusted and welcome. In his presentation of climate-oriented programs, he knows it has to be about what is best for farmers. It must be tested, and it must work. How do you put a price on carbon that works for farmers? There are a myriad of issues that can trip up the climate agenda if not handled right. The backdrop is an agricultural sector that was hurt by a trade war with China. Although US farming is immensely productive, 90 percent of farmers don't make a living farming. They have supplemental income from other jobs and other family members. It takes a side hustle to farm. In the future, could that be them taking a role as a water resource steward or carbon cowboy?

CARBON CREDIT MARKETS AND OTHER INCENTIVES IN THE LAND SECTOR

Chris Adamo, vice president of government affairs for Danone, has a broad perspective on this. He sees climate policy like he's looking out over a rural landscape of farms and forests, keenly understanding how it all fits together like the ebb and flow of the seasons. It's the expansive view of someone who managed the passage of the 2014 Farm Bill. The Farm Bill is one of the tectonic plates of US federal government policy, especially regarding the land sector. It is a package of legislation passed by Congress every five years which sets national agricultural policy that impacts over two million farmers who work nearly nine hundred million acres of land. The agricultural sector is massive. Gross farm income is about $500 billion per year (ERS). The Farm Bill also sets nutrition, conservation, surface water management, and forestry policy. Notably, for the climate change fight, the Farm Bill sets policy for how five to six billion dollars in conservation funding is spent each year. Here, too, the USDA manages nearly two hundred million acres of forests and other federal lands—this is about the size of Texas (US Senate).

As Chris explained to me, one of the biggest targets is to utilize the Commodity Credit Program within the USDA to create a carbon bank that would set a floor price for carbon credits generated by agriculture. This would provide a significant incentive and income support for farmers to adopt regenerative agricultural practices. Robert Bonnie is the new Undersecretary of Agriculture. He was part of a broad study group, the Climate 21 Project, that developed climate policy recommendations across the entire government for the incoming administration. As reported on Agriculture.com, "In his remarks at the Outlook Forum, Bonnie said federal policy could help create new markets for farmers. 'And we can look at a range of policy options, whether it's our farm bill programs, thinking about new creative uses of existing authorities, whether it's a carbon bank, or otherwise, or thinking about how we encourage wood products in the forestry sector'" (Abbott). A great deal of this effort will depend on developing a sound understanding of the carbon removal benefits of agriculture and how to price them.

The markets need to improve—and they are improving. As Chris Adamo said, "It's a non-transparent market right now. There's no place no website you can go to say hey how much for a ton of carbon from a forest." The USDA is set to launch a variety of initiatives to build standards for and jump-start a carbon market for agriculture. The landscape Chris saw bits and pieces of as he began his odyssey is taking shape again. The modeling and the data that goes into models have improved drastically over the last couple of years. "There are good models out there that are getting better such as Comet and DNDC. Those are two big models that can be used here in the US, that capture the full farm picture. Coupling field level data and soil testing with models improves the quantification certainty, the integrity of the outcome," added Chris.

These efforts have challenges, and not everyone is so sure they will work. "'The danger isn't that we'll spend billions of dollars on cover crops, better fertilizer and tilling practices—that's all good—the danger is the government ratifying an offset market that can't yet measure and verify the carbon benefits of those practices, and in doing so allows fossil energy sources to delay the transition to green energy,'" Scott Faber, senior vice president for government affairs at the Environmental Working Group, said in the *Washington Post* when commenting on Secretary Vilsack's confirmation testimony, adding, "'we don't yet have the scientific tools to measure and verify the climate benefits of particular farming practices'"(Reiley 2021). This reframe is a concern throughout the voluntary carbon offset market. It's important to know many of these cropping practices have other benefits as well. They help improve water quality, decrease the risk of floods and droughts, create habitat for other animals, and more.

REGENERATIVE AGRICULTURE AND THE
PRIVATE SECTOR

Meanwhile, the private sector, responding to demand from large corporations for carbon removal services, has jumped in to organize farmers to deliver carbon credits they can sell. There is a growing voluntary market for these services. Companies like Indigo, Nori, Mad Agriculture, Ecosystem Services Market Consortium, and Truterra have entered the market. Quantified Ventures, a Maryland-based impact investing and consulting firm, launched ReHarvest Partners in the fall of 2020, bundling the ecosystem services farmers provide for a variety of stakeholders. These and other companies are building innovative business models in the land sector.

Mark Lambert is emblematic of the new breed of entrepreneurs who don't see any gap between building a business and addressing the public benefits of climate change and other environmental issues. It's a belief grounded in an understanding that maintaining the climate and protecting the environment are foundational values. "Perhaps it's something about my upbringing that sees the moral and existential imperative to address climate change. I think it's hopefully going to be a hallmark of maybe my generation, and certainly the one younger than mine, to focus on these challenges and solve them."

Mark has clearly been focused on solutions to climate change for a long time. His undergraduate thesis was on how to seed the oceans to improve algae blooms to sequester carbon. Bioengineering on this scale and other solutions, such as cloud seeding, have been discussed widely as possible solutions to greatly increase the sequestration of CO_2. These solutions could be relatively inexpensive and easy to implement, but the unintended consequences like moral hazards and geopolitical issues could be huge. In her recent book *Under a White Sky: The Nature of the Future*, Elizabeth Kolbert delves into many of these issues, noting it's a Pandora's Box we should be careful to open. It's evident there are no easy, universal solutions to climate change.

For Mark and others, there is no contradiction in applying business and economic principles to addressing these problems. Markets are human contrivances, and they should represent our values and generate the outcomes we want, taking into account all the costs and benefits. The free market is a phenomenal tool for efficiently applying capital to a problem and creating incentive structures that nudge behavior. Why not make it work for the outcomes necessary to help address climate change, water quality, air quality, or a whole host of ecosystem services? "For my personal career perspective, in any of this stuff, it's always been about trying to leverage markets to help solve climate-related challenges." One thing entrepreneurs, investors, and many policy makers agree on is this potential, and they are working to capitalize on it. As Mark continued, "When markets are harnessed for good, I think there is potential for significant transformative change, and that's really what I've been trying to focus my career on— getting more traditional sources of capital aligned around mitigating climate change."

One innovative solution is to put a value on and bundle together the benefits we get from the environment—the ecosystem services. This makes sense ecologically. Improvements in land use, fisheries management, and forest protection all have multiple streams of benefits for human thriving. Founded by CEO Eric Letsinger, Quantified Ventures is innovating in this area. Collaborating with farmers in Iowa, farming practices that have both water quality benefits and produce carbon sequestration credits are being implemented. Quantified Ventures (QV) facilitates the financial transaction between the beneficiaries of the ecosystem services and the farmers providing them. QV also manages the program to ensure land management practices are adhered to. The city of Cedar Rapids is one of the beneficiaries. Lowering the levels of phosphate and nitrogen in the water supply, Cedar Rapids can forgo the costly installation of sophisticated equipment to process these agricultural pollutants. With a little help, nature can do it cheaper. These same land management practices also sequester more carbon and likely have other benefits as well, such as improving air quality and providing habitat for pollinators. A fuller ecosystem services approach maximizes benefits and income opportunities for the farmers.

Demand from large corporations is increasing rapidly. As we'll discuss in Chapter 13, the voluntary carbon market is expanding. As Mark Lambert continued, "Corporations are making very significant commitments to reduce their greenhouse gas footprints across their entire operation. The prices they're willing to pay to offset these emissions is increasing."

Entrepreneurs are sensing this opportunity and feel they must lead the way. As Mark put it, "We can't wait for governments to step in first. I think we are not going to be well served waiting for policy to come in and be the savior of venture capitalists or investments. Generally, I think you have to go out and demonstrate a market opportunity and show the government exactly where they can provide support, rather than expecting the government to find their way to creation of a market."

It's important to note that many of the project's ecosystem services contracts leverage regulatory conditions that create the need for ecosystem services. For example, drinking water quality standards create the need to pay farmers to change their land management practices. In this case, entrepreneurs are structuring the market incentives to internalize the problem and create opportunities for farmers to benefit.

One of the challenges is the need to measure and quantify the stream of services from a producer. The idea is if you can measure these things and put them into a market context; you create an incentive structure to deliver more ecosystem benefits. As Eric Letsinger said, "It's incumbent on the folks who understand those projects and who are active in this supply chain to create frameworks for that capital to invest. If we don't, we miss a huge opportunity." We try to operate from the principle of being very conservative in our estimates." The measurement, reporting, and verification (MRV) challenge is real and a very active area of innovation and debate in this growing industry (more on this in Chapter 13).

Some companies are trying to address this head-on by providing the technology—a monitoring and data management platform—to enable regenerative agriculture and the reporting required to secure carbon credits. Truterra is one example, and they are providing a soil health planning suite of tools. "TruCarbon is providing farmers new opportunities to be recognized and rewarded for their stewardship, creating new revenue opportunities for farm families as they adopt soil health practices, and increasing the focus on carbon storage in crop fields," said Land O'Lakes chief executive Beth Ford.

With a newly engaged USDA, innovation of entrepreneurs, and increasing demand from large corporations for carbon offsets, this market seems poised to grow. "'It's remarkable to me how quickly all this has occurred,'" says Ferd Hoefner, Senior Strategic Adviser for the National Sustainable Agriculture Coalition. "'In the last two years, many companies have proposed carbon markets or [carbon] policy proposals'" (Gullickson 2021).

SUMMARY

As we will continue to see in the next chapter, the natural world, the biosphere of which we are a part, presents a huge opportunity to mitigate climate change. With better management of the land sector, our farms, forests, and wetlands can sequester more carbon and provide a stream of other benefits. The entrepreneurial market-based solutions described here hold great promise for bringing more capital to the table to improve land use. Like with all things in the natural world, it's super complicated. The promise and the peril go hand in hand.

- Natural areas can either be a source or a sink of CO_2. If managed improperly, the land sector will continue to be a net source of CO_2 into the atmosphere. This would make stabilizing the climate an even steeper climb.

- Verification and incentive programs are complex and costly. More innovation is needed to truly scale to large areas in the order of hundreds of millions of acres in the US alone.
- Local conditions vary widely, and there are lots of different actors. One of the challenges of scaling is creating a framework that can be broadly applied. Regulators can help in this area by enabling standards.

Clearly, part of the climate change issue is we are pushing the limits of the land sector. Modern farming and forestry practices can degrade the land's ability to absorb and store carbon. Market-based approaches to promote new practices hold promise as one part of the solution. The actions and innovation of the entrepreneurs, investors, and policy makers exemplified here are leading the way.

CHAPTER 10

Blue Carbon

"It always brings me back to our broken markets, and every-
thing else rests on that—our societies and our economies sit on
the foundation of a healthy environment, and if that doesn't
go, well, we're screwed."
—KRISTIN RECHBERGER, CEO OF DYNAMIC PLANET

The sentiment from Kristin's quote came up over and over again as I researched this book. It's a recurring theme. We (I mean us—humans) need to reconcile our fit within nature. As discussed in Chapters 2 and 3, we've upset the complex balance in the carbon cycle that created a sweet spot for human thriving. In this Anthropocene world, we need to foster nature's ability to support life—all life—to ensure a feathery nest our own. Perhaps in no place is this more abundantly clear than our ocean ecosystems.

Oceans are massive carbon-sequestering perpetual motion machines. Using the power of the sun and the moon, they fantastically sequester carbon for long-term storage and circulate it into things we love and depend on. Yet humans have become amazingly adept at trashing them. Perhaps worst of all, we've done a lousy job at organizing ourselves well enough to protect them and benefit from them sustainably.

There are fantastic examples and a growing mountain of data on just how powerful ocean ecosystems are and the array of ecosystem benefits they deliver. The ocean and its coastal interface provide an array of benefit streams. These are like service-income lines for a business. They can all be quantified, but not all have hard benefits that fit neatly into our economic system. This is what economists would call a market failure—or an "externality."

Our oceans provide sustenance. Seafood feeds nearly 3.5 billion people every day. Coastal marshes, mangrove forests, sea grasses, kelp forests, and coral reefs all support fisheries. Pelagic (open water) ecosystems also support huge fish populations. The ocean is an energy source through wind, solar, and tidal action. Coastal ecosystems protect shorelines as well as our homes and towns from storm damage. They are a source of genetic diversity, which creates longer-term resilience for the biome. Oceans regulate weather and climate. They detoxify and trap sediments. They provide cultural services, including recreational, educational, aesthetic, and spiritual services. They support economic activity, including jobs, fisheries, food, marine transportation, and trade. Oceans support nutrient cycling and primary production—but you get it! This is just a summary of the array of benefits we reap from the oceans.

All of these benefits can be characterized as a flow of services. These flows have limits. Extract too much the ocean's ability to support the flow is reduced. These flows can support a sustainable amount of consumption. That brings us to carrying capacity. Carrying capacity is defined as the maximum population of a given species that can be supported indefinitely in a defined habitat without permanently impairing the productivity of that habitat. Humans are degrading the carrying capacity of oceans.

OCEANS—VAST, REMOTE, MYSTERIOUS

Many people don't have much experience with the stuff that covers 73 percent of our planet, oceans. Yet, they are inarguably the most important battleground for climate change mitigation.

I grew up in the Midwest. I think the first time I tasted briny ocean water was swimming in the Gulf of Mexico on a family vacation to South Padre Island. I must have been eight years old. I remember throwing pieces of bread off the hotel room balcony with my brother Tom and marveling at the acrobatics of the black hooded laughing gulls as they swooped down to catch the falling prizes. Even now, after twenty or more years of international travel, I've still never been more than twenty or thirty miles from a land mass. I'm a recreational diver, and I spent many nights as a kid glued to the TV watching *The Undersea World of Jacques Cousteau*. Man! I wanted to be him. Even as someone who's pretty curious about the oceans, they seem vast, remote, and mysterious. I'm sure for many, they seem limitless.

It's almost a trope in conservation circles that the oceans are largely unexplored and poorly-understood data voids.

They have been challenging to study. They are dangerous. We need special equipment to spend more than a few minutes below the very thin top layer of the oceans. Humans have spent more time in outer space than we have in the deepest parts of the ocean (Kershner 2021). Today, new technologies, satellite data, remote sensing, and data analysis are changing this reality (Carlyle 2013).

A few years ago, I attended a presentation by Jacqueline Savitz of Oceana at TEDxMidAtlantic, showing the location data from fishing vessels worldwide (Savitz 2019). This simple visualization showed just how overwhelmed the oceans were. There are many thousands of fishing vessels constantly working in the open ocean. Oceans aren't limitless. Nearly every corner of them is directly impacted by human activity. Indirectly, through climate change, plastic pollution, noise pollution, or other effects—no part of the ocean is untouched.

Oceans are not vast blue voids. They are huge, complex, phenomenally productive ecosystems. These ecosystems, and the ocean sediments they produce, are a massive carbon store.

Enter Kristin Rechberger. Kristen is helping drive a wave of new analysis that establishes guidelines for how to manage ocean resources in a way that maximizes these benefits. Implementing these recommendations has proven difficult. The same vastness, extraordinary productivity, and complexity that make oceans such a vital part of the solution makes them very difficult to regulate and manage. Kristin is an unlikely person to be connected to all this ocean stuff.

Born in western New York, Kristen had about as much affinity with the ocean as many Americans, only interacting with them on family vacations. She wasn't a born conservationist, either. Her family was in the cookie business, and that was the natural path for her to follow, but she was interested in more worldly issues. Kristin studied public policy and became animated by how negative mainstream media was. This drove her on a path of documentary filmmaking. With longer-form storytelling, she could uncover the more positive and inspirational stories that resonated with her. Then Kristin was brought back to the US to join *National Geographic* and help build the cable channel. It was a dream job in the capital of inspirational media with the Discovery Channel and PBS, also headquartered in the Washington, DC, area. Kristin thought she'd stay for two years, and it ended up being fourteen great years. Through this time, and then later on the "society side"—the nonprofit arm of *National Geographic*—Kristin's interest in the environment and having an impact really developed. Now Kristin is more focused on impact and the deep understanding that conservation is necessary to support human thriving. Nowhere may this be more important than our oceans.

OCEANS ARE A POTENTIALLY MASSIVE PART OF THE SOLUTION

Oceans are a massive part of the climate solution. They hold fifty times more CO_2 than the atmosphere. Phytoplankton capture 37 gigatons of CO_2, 40 percent of all produced (Chami 2019).

All these solutions hinge on one fundamental set of findings: biodiversity is the key. Healthy ecosystems are fundamentally necessary for us to reap the maximum benefit over time, especially in marine environments where we primarily harvest a wild, uncultivated output. It's important to remember that, in most cases on the open ocean, humans are still hunters and gatherers. Yes, we do it incredibly efficiently, but with few exceptions, we hunt for our sustenance. We do nothing to cultivate or transform the ocean to be more productive for us. This is an important distinction from our farms, forests, and ranches, where we have domesticated and bred the things we harvest for thousands of years. Yes, in coastal areas, there are farmed fish, and some fisheries like the North Atlantic lobster, and mussel and clam fisheries are cultivated in a sense. Mainly we rely on the productivity of the ecosystem itself for the production of our food. Healthy, intact ecosystems are fundamentally essential for us.

The stacked ecosystem benefits, including productive fisheries, adaptation and resiliency benefits, recreation benefits, and climate regulation, are hugely important and undervalued. With conservation, these benefits can be attained faster and in a more cost-effective manner than in most land ecosystems. Simply put, ocean ecosystems are massive and exceptionally productive. Akin to the electrification of our industrial and transportation systems, they are a huge lever in establishing the balance of CO_2 in the atmosphere (Bronson 2017). The solutions that increase the oceans' ability to sequester carbon—protecting whales, restoring shore ecosystems, greater regulation of fishing, and habitat preservation—also have other benefits. These practices can pay for themselves.

BIODIVERSITY IS THE KEY

The linkage between healthy ecosystems—undisturbed, intact, fully-functioning, natural ecosystems—and climate change mitigation has not always been understood from a scientific perspective, or more generally, by the public and policy makers. The climate change movement, brought into broad public understand during the 1990s and early 2000s, took a lot of oxygen out of traditional environmental and conservation concerns. For the environmental community, it was almost like the head and the heart became disconnected. There was a massive amount of attention on the existential threat of climate change. A lot of the discussion around it was, and still is, engineering and energy focused. Kristin said, "It felt like there was a huge amount of focus and expertise being poured into that."

All the effort to protect beautiful places, ecosystems, and species got left behind. The latest research supports what many naturalists have been voicing for decades. Intuitively, we should know healthy ecosystems have greater carrying capacity and are more resilient. Healthy ecosystems sustain more life, including human life. Healthy ecosystems, especially ocean ecosystems, sequester vastly more carbon and put it into long-term storage within the biome and as sediments on the sea floor. Now the head and heart may be coming back together. In the ocean, healthy ecosystems equal healthy returns.

"What's wonderful about this moment now is it's all merging back together." Kristin thinks like a filmmaker and a storyteller. In our discussion, she began talking about the new narratives related to nature-based solutions for climate change mitigation, "which means not just decreasing carbon, but increasing nature." Kristen continued, "These are all real revolutionary new pieces of our narrative that are starting to turn into policy which will eventually turn into financing." In the oceans, new research is showing how much of a payoff there is for healthy ecosystems. In recent years, marine sanctuaries, where there are strict no-catch rules, have been shown to dramatically improve fish stocks in other areas. In turn, this is strengthening local economies and livelihoods that rely on the fishing industry. Years ago, these were difficult arguments to make, but now there is significant evidence supporting this (Sala 2021). But this only scratches the surface of the full meaning.

Within David Attenborough's latest biopic on the environment is an interesting statement that can almost be overlooked. He talks about the loss of our wild places and our biodiversity. Why should we care? (Attenborough 2020). "The living world is a unique and spectacular marvel... Working together to benefit from the energy of the sun and the minerals of the Earth [...] Leading lives that interlock in such a way that they sustain each other. Healthy ecosystems are complex. Complex ecosystems are resilient. Biodiversity supports human life and we've overlooked that for too long." "If we hope to solve climate change, humanity must also address this biodiversity crisis— restoring ecosystems and the creatures that inhabit them."

"The ocean has long been seen as a victim of climate change, but it's also a big part of the solution," says *National Geographic* explorer-in-residence Enric Sala (Gibbens 2018).

The upshot of much of this is that strictly protected marine areas are fantastically productive. Currently, depending on your definition, between 2 and 7 percent of the ocean is protected (Gibbens 2018). New research suggests protecting 30 percent—and not just any 30 percent, but the right 30 percent—could have huge economic benefits for local communities that depend on fishing for their economy. Work by Enric Sala and a large group of scientists recently published in *Nature* shows the way. Reaching this goal will require new policy and funding (Sala 2021)

As reported by the sustainable development media organization iD4D, "According to Sébastien Moncorps, Director of the French Committee of the International Union for the Conservation of Nature (IUCN), States must 'integrate nature-based solutions with quantified targets: protected and restored surfaces, and amount of CO_2 stored.' According to the IUCN, only 20% of national contributions related to forests have established objectives. Among states with coastal ecosystems, less than one in five integrate them into their climate change mitigation measures, and many marine areas listed as protected do not, in fact, enjoy any genuine protection. IUCN is therefore calling for the protection of 30% of land and sea areas by 2030. Only 15% of land area is currently protected, and 8% of marine surface, with divergent surveillance requirements and management policies" (ID4D). Let's look a little deeper at the unusual ways biodiversity helps sequester carbon.

WHALES
Okay, I know it sounds far-fetched, but whales are a primary ally in mitigating climate change.

In *A Life on Our Planet,* Sir Attenborough goes on to clearly explain how a little-understood cycle of migration in the ocean has a massive impact on climate change. As it turns out, it's all about whales. There are only about two million great whales in the ocean. These are the largest species like blue, gray, sperm, humpback, and other types of whales. Yet, they have a huge impact on the oceans' ability to sequester carbon. The World Economic Forum estimates each whale sequesters thirty-six tons of carbon, but this only represents a small part of the ocean's carbon-sucking power that whales help catalyze through what is called the Whale Pump. Increasing the whale population through further conservation efforts could significantly impact carbon sequestration (Chami 2019).

Large whales, and likely other marine mammals and large pelagic predatory fish such as tuna, cycle massive amounts of nutrients to the surface of the ocean. Whales feed at depth, then return to the surface to breathe and poop. Their poop is filled with nitrogen and iron. These nutrients fuel blooms of phytoplankton. Phytoplankton are small photosynthesizing algae (NOAA). "A 1% increase in phytoplankton productivity linked to whale activity could mean the capture of hundreds of millions of tons of additional CO_2 a year, equivalent to 2 billion mature trees, according to the IMF." Phytoplankton are consumed by zooplankton, larger crustaceans, and small fish. These animals migrate deeper to avoid surface predators. Some are eaten; many die—producing an avalanche of carbon-laden organic matter that drifts to the ocean floor. Here the carbon, sucked out of the atmosphere by the phytoplankton, is sequestered into long-term storage. The whale pump brings nutrients to the surface that catalyze a massive natural carbon sink. Whales increase phytoplankton blooms. More phytoplankton means more food for zooplankton. Zooplankton provide food for schools of small fish, which migrate diurnally in the water column. So, the CO_2 captured by the phytoplankton ends up sequestered in the sea bottom. Whales' poop catalyzes the whole system.

"Protecting whales could add significantly to carbon capture because the current population of the largest great whales is only a fraction of what it once was. Sadly, after decades of industrialized whaling, biologists estimate that overall whale populations are now less than one-fourth what they once were. Some species, like the blue whales, have been reduced to only 3 percent of their previous abundance. Thus, the benefits from whales' ecosystem services to us and to our survival are much less than they could be." (Chami 2019)

Furthermore, this forms the basis of amazingly complex and diverse marine ecosystems, the combined biomass of which represents a large carbon sink of its own. An estimated 80 percent of all life is in the oceans (Marine Bio). Studies show this biomass is so massive that the physical action of large fish and marine mammals significantly contributes to the mixing of ocean layers, helping circulate nutrients and oxygen, contributing to ocean currents, previously thought to be primarily driven by large physical forces (Katija 2009). This is terraforming on a global scale. It's the granddaddy of all ecosystem benefits. I guess this shouldn't seem so remarkable. After all, the earth is a water planet; life began in the water. Our oceans teemed with life long before our ancestors figured out how to respire oxygen that wasn't dissolved in water.

It turns out nutrients from large marine mammals are also supportive of coral reefs and other marine ecosystems. In marine sanctuaries where large mammals are present, coral is more resilient and less prone to bleaching events associated with high water temperatures. In some ways, the impact of the preservation of these top-of-food-chain marine animals is analogous to other ecosystems. One example is the return of wolves to Yellowstone, which created an opportunity for other species in the ecosystem to thrive, improving complexity, productivity, and resilience. Wetlands in Yellowstone are being restored by wolves. This story repeats itself over and over again. Healthy ecosystems are complex. They have a lot of biomass. They process and store immense amounts of carbon. Healthy ecosystems have a greater carrying capacity for human life.

SHORELINES—MANGROVES, SEA GRASSES, AND KELP FORESTS

For a longer time, shorelines have been the focus of marine ecosystem conservation and their climate change benefits. In some ways, it's easier to understand. They are closer to home, easier to observe, and the connections between conservation and carbon sequestration seem easier to pin down. Although now, it seems as if protecting large swaths of more open ocean areas and more stringently regulating fisheries may have a bigger payoff. Protecting coastal ecosystems— kelp forests, mangroves, and sea grass beds—does have significant benefits. In fact, a small fraction of coastal ecosystems is most important for climate change. Mangroves, sea grass beds, and kelp forests are only present in certain coastal regions.

Kelp forests are actually algae, functioning via pulling nutrients from the sea and sun from the shallows. Kelp can be found predominantly within temperate tidal environments, mainly in the northern hemisphere. As it grows, it sequesters a tremendous amount of carbon—as much as is emitted from twenty million American homes per year. However, coastal development, pollution, changes in the ecosystem, and other factors have reduced the extent of kelp forests. Ultimately, winter storms and wave action dislodge the kelp from its fast. It then sinks to the bottom or is transported into deep water, where it falls and becomes incorporated into deep ocean sediments (Krause-Jensen 2016). Thus, the carbon sequestered by the rapid growth of the kelp forest is sequestered long-term on the ocean floor.

Some startups are catching on to the carbon-sequestering power of kelp as a nature-based way to generate carbon removal credits. These credits can then be sold to companies trying to achieve their zero-carbon emissions goals. Running Tide is one such company (Benveniste 2021).

"Recovery is still possible—the kelp forests are proof. Along the California coast, marine-protected areas have been established to protect kelp habitats. Fishermen are harvesting excess urchins from the barrens" (Esgro 2020). Scientists are working on developing more heat-tolerant strains of giant algae, and environmental groups are restoring reefs and replanting the sea beds where kelp once grew" (Muth 2019; Fredriksen 2020).

"Of the climate solutions they studied, few delivered more carbon bang per buck than mangroves—lush systems of salt-tolerant shrubs and trees that thrive where freshwater rivers spill into the sea. Though these forests occupy just 0.5 percent of the Earth's shorelines, they account for 10 percent of the coast's carbon storage capacity" (Alongi 2014). After seeing the impact of shrimp farming and coastal development on mangroves and the local communities that depend on them, Alfredo Cuarto created the Mangrove Action Project. He's been sounding the alarm about the loss of mangrove forests for over two decades. He's one of the many people dedicated to raising awareness about mangrove habitat loss and its value in the climate fight (Kaplan 2021). Like with kelp, voluntary carbon credit markets are now being used to help incentivize the rehabilitation of mangroves. In Belize, The Nature Conservancy is working with local landowners on Turneffe Atol to rehabilitate mangrove forests. They are working on estimating the quantity of CO_2 sequestered and establishing a market for it. It's a pilot project that could yield broader results over time.

Likewise, on the coast of Virginia, The Nature Conservancy is working to restore eelgrass beds. Sea grasses are another potential source of significant levels of carbon sequestration. The Virginia Nature Conservancy—working with Virginia Institute of Marine Science, the University of Virginia, and Verra, a non-profit organization that verifies carbon credits—is applying to sell the credits from the carbon sequestered from a restoration project of sea grass beds in the Chesapeake Bay. They estimate the restored sea grass absorbs half a ton of CO_2 per hectare. They have replanted 3,600 hectares of sea grasses in the area (Jones 2021)

Blue carbon projects are becoming more popular and are starting to ramp up rapidly. Verra has issued nearly one million carbon credits (each credit represents the verified removal of one ton of CO_2 from the atmosphere). Demand for these types of credits is growing. Amy Schmid, ecologist and manager of natural climate solutions development for Verra, says, "There's a lot of demand for blue carbon credits." She further states that companies in shipping and tourism are keen to put money back into conserving the landscapes they have an impact on—while offsetting their own emissions. Many of these projects offer win-win-win stories for people, biodiversity, and carbon, which boosts the price organizations can get for their credits on the open market. Corporations, including Geneva-based MSC Cruises and Apple, have been exceedingly vocal about their blue carbon purchases and projects (Jones 2021).

These are just a few examples of the immense amount of work being done to quantify and find a market for the ecosystem services—carbon sequestration in particular—of ocean ecosystems. So, what does all this amount to? The World Resources Institute (WRI), in a report leading up to the IPCC Special Report on the Ocean and Cryosphere in a Changing Climate, estimated with additional conservation efforts, the ocean could sequester about 20 percent of the current CO_2 balance. "Implementing this wide array of ocean-based opportunities could reduce global GHG emissions by nearly 4 billion metric tons of carbon dioxide equivalent in 2030 and by more than 11 billion tones in 2050, compared to projected business-as-usual emissions" (Hoegh-Guldberg 2019).

TRAWLING AND OVERFISHING

Overfishing in general and trawling, in particular, are the biggest part of the problem. These go hand in hand with habitat preservation. Overfishing removes critical components of healthy ecosystems that reduce overall carrying capacity and the ability of the biome to produce the stacked benefits we rely on. Most fisheries of the world are overfished today. There are striking examples of how strict exclusion zones improve catch, and this can happen very rapidly. Ocean ecosystems have an amazing ability to recover rapidly.

Besides being a very effective and destructive form of fishing, bottom trawling, it turns out, is a massive emitter of greenhouse gases. Each year, bottom trawlers scrape huge nets across 1.9 million square miles of the ocean floor. This act disturbs ocean-bottom sediments that contain many tons of sequestered carbon, releasing them into the water column. There, they dissolve. Some are exchanged with the atmosphere. This carbon release acidifies the ocean as well. These emissions are estimated to be equivalent to the global aviation industry's about one billion tons of CO_2 per year, roughly 2.5 percent of the total carbon budget for the world (Einhorn 2021).

So, we're overfishing to the point where we are reducing the ocean's capacity to feed us, reducing its ability to sequester carbon, and creating massive emissions. It seems simple: we need to do better. The economic argument is clear. But how do you create an incentive structure in international waters? It's a classic example of the tragedy of the commons (Einhorn 2021).

INCENTIVE STRUCTURES ARE HARD TO IMPLEMENT

The latest research provides the basis for the economic benefits of supporting market-based solutions to meet some of these requirements. Fifty countries, the European Commission, and now the US have all signed on to the "30 by 30" initiative, which sets a target of preserving 30 percent of the land and sea area for conservation by 2030. Nature-based solutions to climate change are becoming more well-known and understood by a broader audience and more widely adopted. Now we need to put a new marker in the ground as far as where we need to go. Our goal should be for entire natural ecosystems to be fully protected.

The Science-Based Targets Initiative is also a recognition of the science showing these combined benefits. Over one thousand companies have signed up for these goals, and more recently, they've begun to include ecosystem benefits as part of the initiative goals. Currently, more than twenty of the participating companies have also signed up for the ecosystem targets. But how do you create an enduring internalized market value for these ecosystem benefits? Given the myriad of stacked ecosystem benefits and the complexity of how they are delivered, is it possible to create a rational market for them? Or do carbon markets provide just a portion of the financial and policy superstructure necessary to support marine ecosystems?

Is it possible a solution exists in other areas? CANSO is an early-stage example of an effort to create a global sector-based carbon market (CANSO). Like fishing, much of the emissions occur in a physical domain that is difficult to regulate—at sea and in the air. Both are markets with difficult mitigation paths. There is no known alternative to burning fossil fuels for long-haul, large-capacity air travel. Fishing fleets have significant capital invested in current methods and inter-generational emotional ties to the industry that make it hard to change. CANSO promises to create price signals that help move the industry over time and reduce emissions through innovation and offsets. Similarly, changes could be made to significantly reduce the impact of trawling, and a carbon tax could help provide funding to support marine protected areas.

WHERE DO WE GO FROM HERE

Thinking about this throughout the writing of this book, it's no surprise the oceans are in the mess they are in. They are out-of-sight, out-of-mind, vast, mysterious, and seemingly limitless. Most of the ocean exists outside national boundaries and is open territory for exploitation, save for hard-to-enforce international treaties. Only in the last few years, with better tech, have we been able to peer over the horizon. Fortunately, oceans are immensely productive and resilient. The payback for protecting them is enormous and accrues quickly. In novel and surprising ways, like the impact of whales, oceans can be amazingly productive and beneficial. Oceans can be a significant part of the solution to increasing nature's ability to remove more carbon from the atmosphere and, thus, increase the carrying capacity for human activity. The key to doing this is biodiversity. The key to biodiversity is conservation.

CHAPTER 11

Black Carbon

───

"When you get below the surface, climate change is a million more problems. Each one is an opportunity. It's the opportunity to find a solution, to grow a business, and to create a sustainable world."

—MAELLE GAVET, CEO OF *TECHSTARS*

For too long, the perception has been the business community was at odds with climate change. Businesses were actively causing climate change and resisting measures to mitigate it. Indeed, this has been true in some areas. The scene at the start of Chapter 1 illustrates this well. Climate change meant more regulation, more costs, and fewer opportunities. The trend has definitely shifted, and I think it has reached a tipping point where climate change is finding its way into every corner of our economic activity and every corporate boardroom. Motivation is emerging from a variety of sources. As the opening quote indicates, there is a wealth of opportunity here. Climate change also poses a huge risk to the balance sheets and bottom lines of large corporations. The investor community has woken up to this fact.

As I outlined at the beginning of Part 3, in this chapter, I will highlight existence theorems—examples from sector to sector of the new technologies and business models being developed to mitigate climate change. These are proof points that help us believe that it can be done and we can make progress. Some are large-scale, old economy companies pivoting to lower carbon or zero-carbon business models. Some are venture-funded startups. Others are project-financed hard tech companies. Some companies are inventing entirely new business models to take advantage of growing markets for carbon removal and ecosystem services.

A NOTE ABOUT ENERGY

I think it's well established that renewable energy sources will dominate energy production going forward. The recipe has been well reported and developed. Solar and wind energy are now as cheap or cheaper than fossil fuel-based energy production. Required grid-scale energy storage options are being developed, deployed, and scaled. Transmissions grids are being augmented to allow for more flexible flows of power. Smart grid algorithms and equipment are being developed and scaled. Distributed generation and storage are coming online at increasing rates. Financing options to promote the use of renewables are expanding. Given all this development, in many cases, the first step to decarbonizing a system, like a transportation system or production system for a given class of commodities, is to electrify it and make sure the electricity comes from zero-carbon sources. Hydro and nuclear likely play a role here and in the future in perhaps hydrogen or other sources. Decarbonizing energy production isn't a slam dunk, so electrifying as many production processes as possible is the first step.

The complications of decarbonizing the electric supply were highlighted during an interview I had with Bryan Hansen, executive vice president and chief generation officer at Exelon Generation. Bryan is not new at this. He has thirty-three years of experience as a nuclear engineer and business leader in the utility industry. He speaks with an executive baritone, and his sentences feel like precisely simplified math equations. Bryan is also an old friend. We were rowers together at the University of Wisconsin, and he still looks like he could jump in and make a boat go fast.

Our interview was on the heels of the State of Illinois setting a goal to become zero carbon by 2050. This mission has vast implications for Exelon, the state's largest electricity provider. Transforming the end-to-end supply of electricity—the generation, storage, transmission, distribution, and consumption—to a zero-carbon system at Exelon's scale is daunting. Bryan struck an optimistic tone, though, and believes it can and will be done. Bryan went further and said the energy supply needs to be "carbon-free where and when we use it" (Hanson 2021). Carbon credits won't be enough because "in the future, we can't have these plants burning coal and spewing out dirt in impoverished communities."

Bryan says the main challenge is producing and storing zero-carbon electricity that is available on-demand and modernizing the grid so it can handle all these intermittent power sources. "The grid actually has lots of supply, but not when it needs it most." New nuclear technology can play a role here. Bryan is a self-described nuclear "fanatic." He believes there is a role to play for more recent designs, such as that of TerraPower or XEnergy. These aren't the $20-billion,

1,500-megawatt behemoths most of us think of, but smaller, intermittent capacity units that can be combined with storage to fill in supply gaps from renewable energy sources. Bryan thinks we are right on the cusp of seeing a lot more investment in this area and corresponding energy storage. He explains, "The ESG stories and ESG investing that needs to occur ... there is a lot of money out there, as you see, to be invested in sustainable environmental friendly energy."

New energy storage technology is also an essential part of the solution and attracts a lot of investment. Energy Vault recently went public in a SPAC for $1.6 billion. Bryan was quick to point out we need longer-term storage as well. Hydrogen could play a role. We could be using excess capacity during the spring and fall when energy usage is low to generate hydrogen with zero-carbon electricity and then using that hydrogen in the summer and winter to meet seasonal demand.

With this myriad of technology choices and incredibly complex operational considerations, I asked Bryan what he thought the best solution was, and I think his answer is a capstone to one of the central themes of this book: "Our aspiration, Jim, is to have a market construct for these decisions. The outcome we want is carbon reduction, so put a price on carbon and let the market go after it. We have to get the business communities to drive Congress to put a price on carbon, like other countries."

Beyond energy supply, there is lots of work to be done. Humans aren't going to stop eating, drinking, moving, living, and working. In fact, all of those things are going to increase, and we need to find ways to take GHG emissions out of them. So, we need to find better processes that emit less CO2. We need to be more efficient and recycle as much as we can. Then we need to sequester the rest.

THE OPPORTUNITY IS HUGE

"While pandemics are short term, the looming climate disaster is not. So, lastly, I'll repeat my 2019 declaration that the 'world's first trillionaire will be a green-tech entrepreneur.'"

—KARA SWISHER, *NEW YORK TIMES* (SWISHER 2020)

Entrepreneurs have taken notice of the quote above. The scale of the problem exceeds the scale of economic changes we've experienced in the past—think the invention of the internet combined with the Marshall Plan on a global scale. The industrial revolution has been fueled by hydrocarbons—the energy source for every physical aspect of our lives has been coal, oil, and natural gas. It gives us heat, light, clothing, food, entertainment, mobility—everything. Now we must not just break that linkage but also eliminate it in almost every way to come into balance with the carrying capacity of this little blue and white spaceship we ride around on. Our work here must also be done within the next couple of decades. Nicole Systrom, the founder of Sutro Energy Group, has been studying energy and environmental policy for most of her career, going on record stating, "This is gonna require a down to the studs reorganization of our economy, if we are truly going to decarbonize. And, that means that if you are a participant in this economy, you will be affected by that change" (Systrom 2021).

For technologists, entrepreneurs, and investors, this means the massive potential to have an impact and strike it rich. The invention of the personal computer and the internet created Steve Jobs, Bill Gates, Jeff Bezos, etc. The ascendance of climate tech has arguably already created *Saturday Night Live* star Elon Musk, founder of Tesla, and will likely create others.

However, the drive to decarbonize our economy will also create many meaningful opportunities that don't scale to the trillions of dollars or are "investable" in the speak of venture capital and private equity. As said earlier, one of the principles of the change required is all sorts of solutions are needed at all levels. The natural world requires this as well. Humans live in almost every ecological niche possible. We populate those niches in different ways with different adaptations to our local environment. Many local ways to decarbonize and the nature-based solutions to increase carrying capacity will be unique. In development speak, they need to be "context-dependent."

I've read about so many exceptional solutions and stories of the creative, mission-driven people who have started these efforts. Here are the stories of a few of them. It's just a tiny sample. There are thousands, I'm sure. For example, Greentown Labs, a Boston-based accelerator, announced ten startups in one press release in April (Greentown Labs). The breadth and pace of development are expanding rapidly. I only had so much energy, and my publisher would only allow so much time to write about this. They are my existence theorems. They give me hope that *we got this*.

CEMENT AND STEEL

Some large sources of CO_2 emissions are hard to mitigate. Unlike the production of electricity, where we have known zero-emission solutions to meet most of the need, the production of some ubiquitous materials produces lots of CO_2. Cement and steel are the building blocks of the human world, and their production creates a lot of GHG emissions.

Cement, the primary ingredient in concrete, is terrific stuff. Globally, concrete is the second-most used material. Water is the first. Eight percent of global CO_2 emissions come from the production of concrete. In the US, we use six hundred pounds of concrete per person, per year (Gates 2021).

To make cement, you need calcium, which we get by burning limestone in the presence of carbon and oxygen. One of the outputs of the chemical reaction is CO_2. So it's not just the energy input that produces the CO_2; it's the chemical reaction in the manufacturing process itself. So how do we reduce this major emissions source? Innovations in materials science might lead the way.

Researching this issue, I found Elizabeth Gilligan. She's an architect and materials scientist working on solving this problem. Inspired by the challenge of climate change, she started Material Evolution to develop and bring to market a cement product that utilizes recycled waste from the metal and mining industry. It's still in the early demonstration project stages. Still, the promise is to produce a cement alternative that reduces CO_2 emissions by 85 percent and yields concrete that is ten times stronger and five times more durable than conventional products. It's a compelling story. As Elizabeth points out, human history is defined by how we manipulate materials, like the Stone Age, Bronze Age, and Iron Age. "History is all about how we make and build things." The challenge now is to decarbonize how we do that.

Carboncure is another company working to decarbonize the built world. Buildings, their construction, maintenance, and climate control represent a growing proportion of total CO_2 emissions, and the world's building stock is growing and expected to double by 2060. As the pace of decarbonization increases in other sectors, like energy and transportation, the embodied emissions, emissions from the construction, and maintenance of buildings become more significant issues. Carboncure's technology injects captured CO_2 into the process of mixing concrete. Some of the CO_2 becomes mineralized in the concrete, thus removing it from the atmosphere and sequestering it long term. It turns concrete into a carbon sink. It can be retrofitted into any concrete mixing operation and is being done at scale today. It doesn't solve the fundamental problem of CO_2 created from cement production, but every bit counts (Gilligan 2021). Many companies in the materials space are working to eliminate CO_2 emissions or utilize CO_2 in new ways to change the emissions equation.

Steel production is responsible for about 8 percent of global CO_2 emissions. Many other companies are vying to capture the enormous market opportunity for green building materials solutions, and big steel producers are increasingly working to reduce the carbon intensity of their production. Traditionally, steel is produced in blast furnaces or basic oxygen furnaces. This process is what most of us think of when we imagine a big, dirty, smoke-belching steel mill. Iron ore gets combined with coke, a form of coal, to produce steel. This process, which adds carbon to iron to make it strong and flexible, creates a lot of CO_2. In the whole process, about two tons of CO_2 is produced for every ton of steel (Fan 2021)

BF-BOF pathway (71% global production) flow diagram, electricity consumption, and CO_2 emission sources

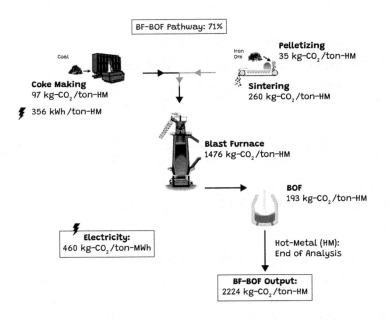

The Steel Making Process

Other less common ways we manufacture steel don't produce as much CO_2, but they are still messy.

There are various methods for reducing CO_2 emissions in steel, and some are being brought to scale. Recycling steel and decarbonizing the energy use is the best method, and it's being implemented extensively now. You avoid much of the CO_2 emissions described above since the steel has already been produced. Big steel companies like ArcelorMittal are now committing to zero-carbon goals by 2050 and are experimenting with new processes for producing steel and capturing carbon emissions from the production stage (Gearino 2020). Currently, companies are regularly ranked and evaluated on their ability to make the transition to low-carbon production (CDP 2019).

CIRCULAR ECONOMY AND WASTE REDUCTION

Not only can we reduce GHG emissions by changing the materials we use, but also by changing how we use and reuse them. In many areas, our economy is immensely inefficient. Some of these solutions could be in the form of clearing-houses or marketplaces that match buyers and sellers better for the reuse of products or waste streams. Others are using materials science to create new uses for waste.

I've traveled to Delhi maybe thirty times from the US. The flights usually arrive late at night. As you leave the customs area and stumble out of the terminal, there is often this familiar smokey smell; it makes me smile. It's a vivid reminder of that gritty, vibrant, amazing place, but obviously, the smoke isn't a good thing. It has a substantial public health cost. Delhi has some of the worst air quality globally; it saps years from people's lives. At least some of that smoke—during certain times of the year—comes from burning crop stubble in farm fields along the river beds and other open areas. After the growing season, you can see the fires and burnt fields traveling between Delhi and surrounding suburbs like Noida and Gurugram.

An Indian start-up called Craste has found a way to repurpose that crop waste into a variety of products. Its estimated five hundred million tons of crop waste are burned in India each year, generating one hundred fifty million tons of CO_2. This refuse can be turned into thousands of other products, including eco-friendly packaging that can also be recycled or composted. The waste also creates an additional income stream for farmers. Craste is an excellent example of a local Indian company servicing a local problem.

Further down the food production system is another company, IXON Food Technologies, which addresses the waste and energy of food transportation and storage. Twenty-five percent of meat and 40 percent of fish and seafood are discarded. This wastage adds up to one hundred million tons of food worth about $300 billion—enough to feed 2.3 billion people. IXON has developed a process of low-temperature sterilization that allows perishable foods to be stored at room temperature for up to two years. This sterilization also eliminates the need for cold chain storage, which saves 80 percent of the energy required for freezing products and 30 percent of the energy needed for canning. This process is in the early pilot stages, but now there are efforts to bring this to scale.

These are just a few examples of the myriad of solutions that will be required to decarbonize our economy and source the sustenance we need. It's worth emphasizing that these solutions have other benefits as well. Along with mitigating climate change, we get cleaner air, improved water quality, more nature, less congestion, and less noise. If we do it right, we aren't just incurring a cost of dealing with climate change; we are investing in a healthier world and improving human development on many axes.

DIRECT AIR CAPTURE

It's probably safe to say all the re-imagining of industrial processes and materials production won't be done at scale by 2050. Some nonpoint sources of GHG emissions will also be stubbornly tricky to eliminate. To top it off, we've injected about 1.2 trillion tons of extra CO_2 into the atmosphere, and we need to take a lot of that out. Nature-based solutions are going to be a colossal lift here. They are available today, at scale, cost-effective, and have all sorts of other benefits. There doesn't seem to be a viable set of solutions that doesn't include much better care of the natural environment. However, direct air capture (DAC) technologies will also likely be part of the solution. Climeworks is one company doing this at a scale that is garnering a lot of investment, along with Carbon Engineering. It's likely for decades to come, these and other companies will find a market providing carbon removal services using renewable energy and various methods to sequester the CO_2 long term to help companies remove the CO_2 they emit.

This will be a recurring playbook across many industries for many years:

- Be as efficient as possible
- Develop new technology to take the GHG emissions out of the process to produce the stuff you make
- Remove the rest from the atmosphere and sequester it long-term.

This brings us to the last point and ties our black carbon story closer to the green and blue carbon stories. As I've said, one of the things we must do to successfully address climate change is to bring our heads and our hearts closer together. The hard black carbon solutions, some of which I've described in this chapter, get us a long way there, but we are going to need a lot of help from healthy ecosystems to get the rest of the way.

CARBON REMOVAL

Some companies are seeing an opportunity to help large enterprises get to "zero."

Jonathan Goldberg is undoubtedly one of those people. Jonathan founded Climate Direct in 2019 to help large enterprises develop and implement plans to decarbonize their operations and structure carbon removal programs for them to counterbalance the emissions they can't eliminate. Jonathan brings a commodity trader's quantitative precision and business zeal to the ad hoc world of voluntary carbon markets and service providers. He says, "We need to manage CO_2

very numerically." A student of energy markets and long interested in the policy and geopolitics of the energy sector, Jonathan is not a striking environmentalist. In the end, to successfully overcome the climate crisis, we need folks like Jonathan. Through his energy work, he became increasingly interested in energy policy, and the overlay with climate policy has become the most extensive area of focus. That was the origin of Jonathan's pivot toward climate policy and carbon removal. "You can see the trend of companies starting to take it seriously." Carbon Direct has created a business model that didn't exist ten years ago.

Carbon Direct advises large-scale enterprises on how to reach carbon neutrality and provides a variety of carbon removal solutions for them to meet that need. It further helps execute and manage these plans for large companies. Carbon Direct is also investing in negative emissions providers, including engineered carbon removal and ecosystem management. Its list of customers is rapidly becoming impressive and includes Microsoft and Shopify.

Driving all of this is a considerable need for decarbonization and carbon removal solutions to meet the goals of the Paris Agreement and bring society to zero emissions by 2050. The scale of the challenge and the opportunity is perhaps unlike anything we've seen before in our economic history.

Quantified Ventures is another company coming at this from a different direction—but, in many ways, the intent is the same. How can we set up financing structures that help investors take the risk to implement ecosystem services to help them meet their emission reduction goals?

These firms are examples of a business model or set of models that didn't exist until recently. From an economic point of view, they are curing a market failure. They are internalizing the externality of CO_2 emissions and helping their partners internalize the cost of paying for the ecosystem services to remove that pollution from the atmosphere. In doing so, they are raising the price of that pollution and creating a market for ecosystem services that have long been undervalued public goods.

EXISTENCE THEOREMS

In Chapter 3, I made the perhaps heretical statement that "We can do this." In some ways, it's a leap of faith. We have no choice. We must; therefore, we will. That is definitionally optimistic. I'm sure some would say I'm naïve, or even worse. I do believe the examples here and countless others I could fill many books with are the existence theorems that show the possibility of a future where we balance our GHG budgets, reduce the CO_2 concentration in the atmosphere, and come into better balance with the climate system. The push toward zero-carbon product systems is everywhere now. I'm surprised by the optimism, but not everyone is surprised. It was summed up well in an interview with Dr. Peterri Taalas, director-general of the World Meteorological Organization: *"Dr. Taalas, you sound optimistic." "Yes, because I've been following this since the 1980s... Now we see the ambition to implement when it comes to countries, to major private sector actors, and to the financial sector."*

CHAPTER 12

Gold Carbon

———

"There is a several trillion-dollar investment gap per year. As a global community, we need to step up and fill this gap to get through the transition we must make. There's room for many more assets to come into this space and help move us along."
—NICOLE SYSTROM, FOUNDER, SUTRO ENERGY GROUP

As countries and companies have mobilized to address the climate challenge, the infusion of capital of all kinds at all levels has expanded dramatically. Just like the response to mitigate climate change is remaking our built world, it is also transforming and refocusing our financial systems. As Jonathan Goldberg put it during our interview, "We need to create a whole system of financing from early-stage to growth equity to project finance to support all this" (Goldberg 2021). Environmental issues and their impact on company income statements and balance sheets are now mainstream. Venture capital investment under the banners of climate-tech, clean-tech, and environmental-tech is booming. Project finance and debt financing models are being innovated. A price is being put on carbon, and emissions permit trading markets are maturing. Yes, there are problems in these areas, but that's the nature of action-led innovation.

ESG INVESTING

Environmental, social, and governance (ESG) investing has become mainstream. Born out of the socially responsible investment movement that began in the 1980s, ESG investing started in the early 2000s and has recently gained momentum. There is a lot of emphasis on the "E" as climate change becomes a huge concern for the valuation of public company assets and risks associated with their profit and loss statements. The first sentence of the CFA Institute (training and certification organization for certified financial analysts) research report on "Climate Change Analysis in the Investment Process" reads, **"Climate change will be one of the most economically impactful events in human history"** (Orsagh 2020).

ESG investing has boomed in recent years. Investment in ESG mutual funds more than doubled in 2020 with $51.1 billion in net new investment. This was the fifth annual record in a row. ESG investing now makes up one-quarter of all investment in US mutual funds, up from just 1 percent in 2014 (Iacurci 2021). The number of sustainability funds available to US investors has also significantly expanded. In 2020, over four hundred investment funds were available. The year 2021 may see ESG investing double again as Q1 inflows were over $21 billion alone. As the track record of these funds becomes clear and access expands to more pension and 401(k) investors, inflows will likely continue to rise. Although ESG investments in the US amount to $17 trillion, about one-third of all professionally managed assets, just 3 percent of 401(k) plans, have ESG investment options. This is due to a myriad of legal and US Department of Labor regulatory rules that have become a bit of a political football. These policy choices matter. The 401(k)s have $9 trillion in assets. Nonetheless, the drive toward ESG investing has a real impact and is based on concerns of the viability of traditional investments in a world increasingly impacted by climate change. "Today we remain convinced that continuing to invest in fossil fuels poses an unacceptable financial risk to UC's portfolios and therefore to the students, faculty, staff and retirees of the University of California," Jagdeep Singh Bachher, the university's chief investment officer, said (Iacurci 2020).

Perhaps there has been no finance industry executive more vocal about the centrality of ESG investing than the CEO of BlackRock, Larry Fink. BlackRock is the world's largest investment management firm with about $9 trillion in assets under management. BlackRock introduced ninety-three new sustainability solutions in 2020 (BlackRock). As a substantial index investor, BlackRock's positions on investment risk, corporate governance, and other issues are pertinent to the CEOs of large public companies that inevitably make up a commensurate proportion of BlackRock holdings. Mr. Fink's annual letter to CEOs has become a must-read over the last couple of years, highly notable for its focus on climate risk as investment risk. "We know that climate risk is investment risk. But we also believe the climate transition presents a historic investment opportunity" (Fink 2021).

It's fair to question the investment community's commitment to ESG investing and its impact on creating real climate progress. Larry Fink and BlackRock have been criticized for not ridding their portfolios of fossil fuel companies. They are the largest investor in fossil fuel companies. BlackRock's Big Problem is an environmental advocacy campaign trying to influence BlackRock and the rest of the ESG investment community to do more and to do it faster (BlackRocksBigProblem). There are significant questions about whether or not ESG standards are moving the needle on sustainability. One counterpoint to the divest argument is the recent proxy fight over the ExxonMobil board of directors nominees. BlackRock and others sided with activist investors to reject the ExxonMobil managements nominees for the board in favor of more environmentally conscious nominees—and they won. Staying invested makes this kind of influence possible. This still seems like amazing progress. Less than ten years ago, these types of investment considerations were niche at best and considered anti-business at worst. Now the investment community seems to grasp the risk and the potential benefits.

The rise of ESG investing and new reporting requirements do seem to be having an impact. As Eric Waeckerlin put it in our interview, "I'm not an SEC lawyer. I'm a Clean Air Act lawyer, but you know, my clients, which are mostly large oil and gas companies, are paying a lot of attention to the SEC stuff." Later he continued, "The companies I work with are great at working within the federal and state regulatory environment. These are heavily regulated industries, and they have decades of experience dealing with environmental regulations. But these activist investors are a new phenomenon that's creating a lot of action." In the past, the investor community might have been more well-aligned with management. This alliance seems to be breaking down. Investors are worried about business models that are heavily dependent upon emitting CO_2. Asset valuations are at risk. The cost of capital for these companies increases as investors reassess risk and rebalance their portfolios away from high carbon business models. It's not all altruistic either. Companies see a significant business opportunity in repositioning themselves for a zero-carbon world. The oil and gas companies that are a prominent part of the economy in the western US are no different. "Vicki Hollub, the CEO of Occidental, you know they're one of the biggest operators here in Colorado and they're all over the world. They're huge. She said she considers that company to be in a carbon management company" (Waeckerlin 2021). They see the opportunity in utilizing their capabilities for carbon capture and storage as well.

As Larry Fink detailed in his most recent CEO letter, "As the transition accelerates, companies with a well-articulated, long-term strategy and a clear plan to address the transition to net zero will distinguish themselves with their stakeholders—with customers, policymakers, employees and shareholders—by inspiring confidence that they can navigate this global transformation" (Fink 2021). This seems like a good segue to the venture capital segment of the financial puzzle.

VENTURE CAPITAL

There is a Techstars video of Cody Simms teaching a class of shiny young entrepreneurs about what they need to have ready as they reach out to potential venture capitalists (VCs) for funding. He calls it the Mise en Place, inspired by the

French culinary phrase—with the main point being entrepreneurs should have all of their necessary fundraising materials prepared before starting the fundraising process. It's a sun-filled room with sleek, glassy furniture, and he's talking relaxed and fast in a clear, organized, and eternally optimistic way of entrepreneurs and investors—confident, friendly, organized, and efficient. His hair and beard are shaved close. He's dressed in an appropriate version of the "California tech investor uniform"—jeans, untucked shirt, sneakers.

Techstars is a behemoth when it comes to incubating and investing in early-stage technology startups. As of 2019, they had accepted over 1,600 companies into their programs at numerous campuses around the US and major cities worldwide. Originating from Boulder, Colorado, they have subsequently fanned out and partnered with major companies, launching campuses in major commercial hubs focused on big investment themes of the day, including communications, music, aging, energy, and sustainability. It's easy to be excited and hopeful about the prospects for addressing climate change when Cody talks about all the different ways companies within their ecosystem are working on these problems.

"The optimism is the sheer number of different types of solutions right now, so it's a cop-out answer, because it's not like there's a magic bullet solution." Techstars is involved in developing solutions to climate change issues across a range of fronts. Today they have six different accelerator programs that touch on the issue. One of their sustainability-focused business accelerators is in their HQ city of Boulder, Colorado, in partnership with The Nature Conservancy. Business accelerators and incubators are sort of like maker spaces for entrepreneurs. If you have a promising early-stage business or product, you can apply to a program like Techstars, where you receive investment and join a cohort of other entrepreneurs. It's highly selective, but if you are invited to participate, you will be bathed with outside expertise and mentorship from product marketers, engineers, management experts, and others. These experts help refine your business, dramatically accelerating your progress, which in turn helps attract more funding to cover the next leg of development.

Most of the companies coming through the Techstars Sustainability Accelerator in Boulder are focused on nature-based solutions to climate and sustainability. Among its other climate and sustainability-oriented accelerator programs, Techstars also has an energy program in Birmingham, Alabama, which is partnered with Alabama Power—all of which fall under the umbrella of The Southern Company. Additionally, it operates another energy-focused program in Oslo, Norway, that's in partnership with the energy giant Equinor. Techstars Farm to Fork in Minneapolis is focused on food and agriculture systems and is in partnership with Cargill and Ecolab. Techstars has a materials sciences—focused accelerator program with the Heritage Group in Indianapolis—as well. Across the Techstars portfolio, there are roughly two hundred companies addressing sustainability and climate issues. It's an impressively dizzying array of innovation and investment. The scope is hard to capture as Cody rattles off the list of companies, programs, and solutions to different parts of the vast constellation of problems that must be addressed on the path to a zero-carbon future. Cody is clearly passionate and amazingly informed as he coordinates these efforts for Techstars in his role as SVP of climate and sustainability. He's the perfect mix of calm and urgent. The journey of a Kansas kid to climate change practice leader is an inspiring one.

In 2019 he was contemplating a move to China to launch Techstars there. "I stopped and reflected on that in January of 2020. I came to the realization climate change was this huge looming thing I'd read a lot about and had some cursory understanding of but hadn't fully stopped to contemplate how much it was going to affect the entire global economy." Cody goes on in his cascade of thoughts. You can feel how he must have been grasping the enormity of the challenge for the first time. "I just decided to lean in fully, not knowing where it would go, but I just assumed industries as large as energy, agriculture, transportation and mobility, manufacturing, property, and real estate all are going to face these impacts. And, you know, potentially up to twenty percent of the world's landmass in the next fifty years will become too hot to live on." It started to click together for him, and with the zeal and clarity of an entrepreneur, he leaned in hard.

Cody continued: "Another realization I had that helped me build conviction around going all-in on climate was seeing how well many of our purpose-led portfolio companies did during the earliest days of the COVID-19 pandemic. While many startups struggled in those first few days of lockdown, a number of the companies that were working on something bigger than the bottom line were all doing very well. It helped me realize when you invest in things that matter to the world, they're more resilient investments. They're not only good in terms of their purpose, but they have financial longevity."

Cody found the purpose-driven investments in the Techstars portfolio were doing very well. Companies with impact do better. One of them was WELL Health, a digital communications platform that allows for patients and health systems to communicate with each other bi-directionally via text. They just took off during COVID-19. Another company Tasso, Inc., is a micro blood collection device that allows patients to do at-home phlebotomy work. The third company is called Voatz, a mobile voting solution using blockchain and saw a lot of adoption during the last voting cycle when everyone was trying to access the polls and stay safe. "So, all three of those companies helped me realize when you're investing in technologies that are world positive, it pays dividends in hard times and everything I was reading about climate change was causing me to realize we were coming on to potentially significantly hard times" (Simms 2021).

Dots connected; Cody dove in. He joined the My Climate Journey (MCJ) community to learn more about climate change, the technology and business models employed to make an impact. Cody researched the full breadth of all the climate and sustainability-related investments across the Techstars network. Cody took a twelve-week course from the Terra.do learning community. Both MCJ and Terra.do, in their own right, are great examples of the mission-driven impact-oriented climate entrepreneurship that is snowballing. These gave him the grounding in the science and policy details of climate change. That was the springboard for him to launch Climate Changemakers during the 2020 election. Climate Changemakers is a virtual community of climate change activists with the simple goal of organizing collective political action for one hour a week. During the election, it was primarily focused on US Senate races. Now they focus on getting folks like you and me to spend an hour a week advocating for climate legislation that matters during one of their three hourly sessions per week, which place across the US and Europe, while also supporting climate-friendly candidates for federal office.

The Clean Tech Climate Tech movement is gathering momentum. It seems impossible to keep up with growth in venture activity in this area. It also appears to be a much more decentralized movement than the venture-fueled tech booms of the past. At times, the Silicon Valley venture and tech community has been famously blasé about impact, purpose, ESG, and the like. There is a solid libertarian vein of thought that has dominated there. It's somewhat new ground for the venture tech community to gravitate toward the messy, big, hard tech infrastructure types of initiatives needed in many cases to address climate change. Investment needs are enormous, and payback periods can be drawn out. But the number of investors and funds springing up focused on climate change is exploding. Investors like Sierra Peterson, Chris Sacca, and Clay Dumas all have investment platforms. Sophie Purdom published the *Climate Tech VC* weekly newsletter and kept a burgeoning list of the venture funds in this market.

However, there may be limits to what venture investing can do to mitigate climate change and foster carbon markets. Cody describes two big categories of entrepreneurship that need to be invested in separately. "There's what we would classically call clean tech—the stuff the venture community typically looks at—which is singular breakthrough technologies that have the potential to get to global scale and solve problems in a large way. That's your traditional venture model where you're going to aim for unicorns. You're going to write checks and expect large-scale multiples, and that will continue to happen. There's an explosion of that right now." There are new solutions being invented that address parts of the problem, whether that be grid resiliency, new forms of renewable energy, energy storage, hydrogen, block-chain accounting for carbon credits, and countless other globally scalable platforms being developed right now.

Techstars is part of this growth in global north tech solutions to help decarbonize the economy. Cody fires off a list of promising new companies. Hyperion energy is helping sequester carbon from industrial processes and converting it into usable waste streams. Opus Twelve is converting CO_2 into industrial chemicals; Ampair is developing electric airplanes; Nori is using blockchain to do soil sequestration accounting; Pixxel is developing hyperspectral satellite imagery for CO_2 flux monitoring, which they can accomplish today using drones. The sheer volume and variety of investments are impressive, and you can't help but be encouraged. The enthusiasm and energy are infectious.

One of the things I think makes some people wary, or even put off, by the venture and entrepreneurial communities is their total lack of impostor complex. Cody's story of waking up eighteen months ago and deciding that climate change was the existential threat of our time can no doubt be perceived with a "WTF" shrug by climate scientists, environmentalists, and policymakers that have been sounding the alarm since before the IPCC was formed nearly forty years ago. To be honest, though, does it matter? There is a need for everyone with imagination, energy, and purpose, whether they found it yesterday or a generation ago. The zeal and organizational skills of the entrepreneurial community should be embraced. Many of these people know what it takes to rapidly mobilize resources to scale solutions globally. They've built and run billion-dollar companies. They know how to market and sell. These are needed skill sets in the climate fight. I have to say, all the folks in this sector I've talked to over the course of writing this book have impressed me with their sincere passion for creating positive change. They also believe in the clear signal of the profit motive, and indeed the first trillionaire may be in climate-tech.

There is another wave of investment need that doesn't fit this model. Much of the mitigation, resiliency, and adaptation solutions will be locally specific. For example, better water management systems in India to conserve water so as the monsoon fluctuates, communities can be better prepared, or solutions for coastal and island communities dealing with sea-level rise. Solutions for climate migration, building efficiency solutions—all of these require investment, but they don't scale as rapidly or globally as traditional VC investment requires. Is there a for-profit model that can help foster these types of mitigation and adaptation investments that could be a massive part of the solution? Is this where staked ecosystem benefits and markets for these services comes in? Cody continued, "I'm trying to see if I can figure out, given the global seat I sit in, from an early stage investment perspective. Are there new investment models we can use, whether it's revenue-based financing, public benefits corporations, or co-op structures that can lock in a multiple (an investment return) on an investment, but allow ownership structures to be maintained by the founders and employees of the company?" So, this is the new quest and certainly a considerable part of the broader story on carbon sequestration markets and solutions to the climate crisis. VC is notably bad at being patient developing high-CAPEX, long-term solutions to problems. This shortcoming is where another part of the financial model needs to fall into place: project finance and merchant banking.

PROJECT FINANCE

Big infrastructure projects often require a different kind of financing. Longer-term debt financing, including environmental impact bonds and other types of project finance, are necessary. This type of financing may be more backed by income streams than by equity, but it takes a lot of different forms.

Jigar Shah has been engaged in many of these initiatives over nearly two decades. Jigar popularized a way of turning capital hardware investment into an investible income stream through a power purchase agreement where customers could benefit from solar power infrastructure without having to make the capital investment. The income stream could be used to finance the capital expense, pay for project management, and provide a return for investors. This was a novel take on the Hardware as a Service (HaaS) pricing arrangements typical in some other industries. At Sun Edison, Mr. Shah pioneered this approach in the solar industry. One of the challenges going forward is how this model could be employed in many other sectors of the economy necessary for the transition to a zero-carbon economy. "Infrastructure, climate solutions. So, when you think about when we talk about project finance, that includes everything" (Shah 2020).

Jigar went on to form Generate Capital to work on this problem specifically. How can project finance be applied to different sectors that need to decarbonize where technical solutions exist and can be scaled? We need to finance the deployment of new infrastructure. This is a big part of the overall financial model, whether it's anaerobic digesters, power storage, transportation. There are many options for income-based infrastructure finance that can speed the path toward decarbonization. In some of these industries, like solar, VC makes up only a small percentage of total investment in the sector, so you need project finance to continue to make progress.

Jigar has now been appointed as the director of the Loan Programs Office at the US Department of Energy, where he is working on deploying these ideas and creating the regulatory framework to further expand investment in new infrastructure.

Ricardo Bayon, who I first introduced in the Introduction, has also pioneered another form of project finance that looks much more like a merchant bank. In areas like carbon sequestration programs, structured finance is needed to provide the capital necessary to establish the forest land management practices to establish the offset. This requires a bespoke form of structured finance. At EKO, Ventures Ricardo raised a fund, like a VC, but then created the land management agreements with landowners, got the carbon credits certified, and sold them, providing a return for investors. Again, it wasn't a VC-oriented equity play.

CONSERVATION FINANCE

One of the reasons for writing this book and for its scope (I sometimes think I bit off more than I can chew) is to connect a bunch of dots between different sectors and actors of this problem that don't necessarily see each other. The diverse world of conservation finance plays an important role here and dovetails with the type of carbon offset financing Ricardo developed. We typically think of ecological preservation as being something that can only be funded by governments, but the market for private conservation finance in the US is very large. Each year there is over $4 billion in wetland and stream restoration alone that is done by private companies (Bloomberg 2021).

Perhaps what's unique about conservation finance is the role government can play to create opportunities to draw in more private sector funding. Changes in these policies can attract more private sector funding. Many of these mechanisms involve creating markets for environmental benefits of compliance with environmental regulations. For example, in Pennsylvania, a revolving water fund run by i2 Capital—led by founder and CEO Ashley Allen Jones—has been set up that pays farmers to restore water quality. The credits from farmers are bought by others to meet regulatory requirements. There is a myriad of financial structures to incentivize private investment in conservation.

CARBON MARKETS

As simple as it seems, putting a price on CO_2 emissions has been politically fraught and technically challenging. As we discussed in Chapter 2, markets for SOX and NOX were created in the US with relative ease back in the 1980s, so why has it been so hard to do it with CO_2? CO_2 emissions are global and emitted from almost everything, including us. The linkage to climate change has not always been widely understood, and the impacts are far more removed in time and space from the emission. This being said, after all sorts of efforts and fine-tuning, the activity of the largest emitters in the world is now covered by a carbon market. Even the US, where any form of tradeable emissions permits a cap-and-trade system or other forms of market mechanisms to put a price on CO_2 emissions, has been a contentious political battlefield where such markets cover a large chunk of the country.

Transparency, liquidity, and accountability are part of the proper function of any commodities market, and improving those has been a considerable challenge. The EU carbon market was challenged with a flood of poorly verified carbon credits early in its history that drove down the price of offsets. It also called into question the efficacy of the market to constrain emissions. Companies could cheaply offset their emissions and not have to reduce their own emissions. Most of the offsets have been found to be of poor quality.

Nevertheless, markets are expanding and becoming better organized. In the US, thirteen of the biggest states are covered by a carbon market. In California, the California Air Resources Board (CARB) operates a cap-and-trade market there. In the eastern US, the Regional Greenhouse Gas

Initiative (RGGI) funds conservation and emissions reduction projects through proceeds of its cap-and-trade system for large emitters. Virginia was the most recent state to join RGGI. There is also a voluntary market that has gone through many ups and downs over the years. The Chicago Mercantile Exchange (CME) had an active exchange. Then they shut it down, and emissions trading has been conducted strictly through bilateral private arrangements on a voluntary basis.

Carbon markets continue to grow. Based on the WB study, they were bringing in $82 billion from the global market in 2019 and $18 billion in 2018. Though, some estimates place the figure from 2019 as being over $100 billion. Now the CME has relaunched its market. "'It is a brand-new market for many players,'" Peter Keavey, global head of energy at CME Group, told Reuters. "'We can help provide standardized pricing benchmarks and improve price discovery in the voluntary offset market. That's our goal.'"

Some global standards are also coming into view that might create a precedent for global exchange. The aviation industry has a problem with emissions that's very hard to solve. CORSIA (Carbon Offset and Reduction Scheme for International Aviation) is a model for helping the aviation industry deal with these hard-to-remove emissions. It could also be a model for a global market to account for supply chain emissions across many different sectors, such as shipping.

Finally, China and the UK launched their markets, too. China's market immediately became the largest in the world. The detailed chart below shows the breadth of the push to regulate carbon emissions.

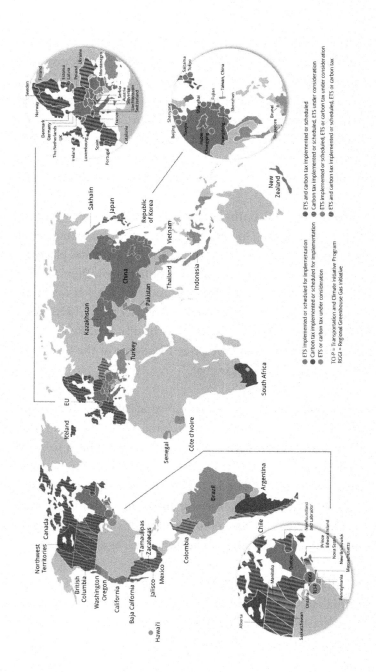

THE PATH FORWARD

As climate change mitigation transforms how we eat, shelter, move, reproduce, play, and die, it also reshapes the financial systems underpinning these activities. Nature's ability to sustain these activities is being priced in. Effectively, a market failure in economic terms and externality is being internalized. The cost of using the atmosphere as an open sewer for GHG emissions is being factored in more and more.

CHAPTER 13

Estimation and Verification

———

"As a hedge fund manager, if you say you made a 10 percent return, you have to verify that you made it. There is no ambiguity. In the carbon offset market, it was like anything goes. You can make any claim you want. There's no verification and the durability of the offset doesn't have to be there [...] we need to manage CO2 very numerically."

—JONATHAN GOLDBERG, CEO OF CARBON DIRECT

Lucky number thirteen. This may be the hardest chapter of this book to get right. Jonathan's quote is a bare-bones critique of carbon offsets, and it represents one frequency range in a spectrum of views. I hope to tell the whole story here. Getting this right is important. In the introduction, we needed a new form of environmentalism that actively and continuously accounts for the benefits we reap from nature. This is where the rubber meets the road. Many climate change mitigation solutions, especially nature-based ones, depend upon our ability to accurately account for the sequestration benefits in a market context. Doing this on a small scale is difficult. Just like in other areas, we need to innovate and improve the measurement, reporting, and verification of carbon sequestration programs so we are sending the right market signals and we are paying for results. I'll try to give a fair representation of a range of perspectives below. It's funny, but the naive idea to write this book started here.

Some years ago, when the company I worked for called WeatherBug changed its name to Earth Networks and launched what we hoped would be a global network of GHG monitoring systems. The need seemed clear. Governments and companies were going to have to reduce GHG emissions. They would need to monitor the air resource. We'd need to know more than the global mean level over time, like what is measured at the observatory on Manu Loa HI for the Keeling Curve I talked about in Chapter 3. We'd want to see the minute-by-minute fluxes on a scale small, enough to see point source changes and emissions from all the daily non-point sources and sinks. Ultimately, we will want to see a signal in all this noise that our efforts to reduce GHG emissions and increase GHG sequestration are resulting in lower concentrations of CO_2 in the atmosphere. As it turns out, it's hard.

More than ten years later, Earth Networks operates regional networks of GHG sensors deployed on tall radio towers in the US. The data is used as part of a research program with the National Institutes of Standards and Technology (NIST). NIST is a fascinating and surprisingly important agency within the US Department of Commerce. They develop standards and measures for all kinds of things. We don't think about it every day, but what would happen if there wasn't a standard for how long a foot was, or the mass of a kilogram? Trade and commerce would stop. Building stuff, exchanging goods—all the day-to-day activity we depend on—would be nearly impossible. Similarly, if we need to get mathematical and rigorous about how we manage GHGs, we might need NIST to help sort out the details of how we quantify sources and sinks. Can we accurately measure the fluxes in atmospheric concentrations and track down their origin? NIST has a program attempting to figure this out.

James Whetstone, PhD, is the special assistant to the director of the Greenhouse Gas Measurements Program. He's at the forefront of tackling this problem. Dr. Whetstone is an amazingly amiable person. He's tall and quick to smile. Despite decades in the Washington, DC area, he still speaks with a slow southern cadence that makes you feel like you are on a front porch sipping sweet tea while talking about measurement complications of sniffing the atmosphere at parts per billion. This program seeks to advance the science, standards, and methodologies supporting greenhouse gas measurements. He has established multinational collaborations and investigations in partnership with other federal agencies, industries, and academic institutions. Additionally, he is active within the greenhouse gas measurements communities both in the United States and abroad. He is a frequent speaker at conferences and enables dialog among a wide range of communities with research interests in measurements (NIST).

Prior to this appointment, he was chief of NIST's process measurements division, where he was responsible for research ranging from advances in contact and remote sensing technologies to the development of new approaches to the realization of measurement standards for temperature, pressure, relative humidity, and flow rate. He sees these measurement challenges as fundamental. He also has a long view. As he put it in our discussion, "The intervening time from 2010 to 2020 has given the science community an opportunity, largely I think through the combined efforts of NIST and Earth Networks, to develop a level of practicality in making these measurements that didn't exist in 2010. I'm encouraged by the possibility we're almost to the place where we know enough to make really significant progress on measurement and verification" (Whetstone 2021).

As you can imagine, the work is complicated. CO_2 is the primary way carbon is moved around the biome. It's emitted and sucked up by almost every living thing and is a part of countless organic processes on earth. Emissions are estimated in several ways. Traditionally, organizations like the US Environmental Protection Agency (EPA) do "bottoms up" analysis by looking at lists of large emitters, like power plants and steel mills, monitoring how much fuel they burn or raw materials they use, and then calculating the CO_2 output. They can also estimate emissions from cars, homes, and other diffuse sources of GHG's by looking at how much gasoline is purchased in an area, how many vehicles are registered, how many miles are driven, and so on. These are typically called "inventories." It's how an accountant would estimate CO_2 emissions, and it works well, except it doesn't physically measure or observe actual CO_2. It doesn't count all the molecules.

In a recent study, NIST is now showing they can come close to reconciling the bottoms up estimates of emissions, through inventories, with the "top-down" measurement of an atmospheric monitoring network, like the one operated by NIST and Earth Networks. Over time, this could lead to a better understanding of sources and sinks, the sequestration benefit of various activities, and a clearer market signal (Yadav 2021).

So, it turns out measuring GHG concentrations is not that hard (at least today—it was horribly difficult decades ago when Dr. Keeling first started trying to do it...remember innovation). Doing it at scale in real-time in a very standardized and reliable way is challenging. Regressing these measurements back to sources and sinks at a regional or local level, and tying them back to bottoms up carbon footprint models, is very challenging. Although global math might be straightforward, sectoral math at a local level is hard. The exact quantities of emissions, especially for non-point source emissions, are hard to determine. Every mammal that is breathing and digesting, every house with a gas furnace, most cooktops, and most tailpipes produce CO_2 or methane in some quantity. It mixes in the atmosphere and gets sucked up by anything with chlorophyll. It's a complex mix of stuff. It's very tough to tie all that activity back to measurements at a network of individual points, but the measurement continues to improve. Action is driving the necessary innovation.

The challenge of measuring emissions and calculating sequestration is a central problem for the math of the planet. It's
also a great example of how a bias toward action and the
process of innovation can take us forward. In some ways, it's
early innings in this game. It looks ugly. The measurements
are bad. The math doesn't pencil out. Verification is expensive and doesn't scale. Projects to sequester more carbon are
promising, but questions remain. However, there is significant progress on all these fronts.

MARKET NEED GROWING FAST

As I write this, the demand for carbon credits is booming
(Chestney 2021). The total value of the carbon market jumped
20 percent in 2020. This happened during the pandemic year
when global emissions dropped, and carbon prices hit record
highs. In the US, the two largest markets, The Western Climate
Initiative and the Regional Greenhouse Initiative (RGGI), grew
by 16 percent. Things are set to grow even faster with China's
market coming online. As reviewed in Chapter 12, demand
from companies in anticipation of increased pressure from
governments, consumers, and the general public to curtail
emissions is driving this demand. Commitments from companies, municipalities, alongside other entities, are accelerating.

The Science Based Targets Initiative continues to grow. The SBTi
framework involves the companies quantifying and developing
specific plans for eliminating or offsetting their Scope 1, 2, and
3 emissions. These scopes refer to the different parts of a business operation. Generally speaking, Scope 1 is operations you
own and control, like your manufacturing facility and office
operations. Scope 2 is the energy your company consumes, like

electricity, steam, heating, and cooling. Scope 3 is the hardest part. It includes all the indirect emissions in your company's supply chain. This can include transportation as well as the utilization and disposal of your products. As we discussed in previous chapters, Race to Zero is a UN-sponsored public relations initiative to rally together pledges from corporations and cities. The Amazon Climate Pledge is also attracting more large companies, with over one hundred companies signed up. Amazon is backing it up with investment to support the development of technologies to reduce carbon emissions.

As demand increases, more market entrants are getting into the game. The NASDAQ acquired an emerging carbon credit market Puro.earth. In doing so, NASDAQ positions itself to be more ready for the growing demand of ESG investors.

Recently two additional carbon credit ETFs have been launched to capture the rise in carbon credit commodity prices. These are very nascent and small, yet tangible steps forward (ETF.com). Secretary of State Kerry, who is now the Special Presidential Envoy for Climate Change in the Biden administration, is backing one of these ETFs in a small way (Bell 2020). All of this is just further evidence of the pressing need for advancements in MRV—the measurement, reporting, and verification of carbon sequestration benefits. Carbon accounting will be king.

OFFSET MY EMISSIONS

I got a sense of some of this complexity when trying to offset the CO_2 emissions of my own family. Depending on which service I looked at and what assumptions I made, I got radically different estimates of my own personal carbon footprint. These seemed to be estimations, at best. I looked at many different providers, from Carbon Footprint, TerraPass, and others. Some of them didn't try to take into account details of my lifestyle that could have a significant impact on my emissions. What is the climate where I lived? What do I eat? How big is my home? What do I keep the thermostat set at? Where do I get my electricity? What kind of car do I drive? Perhaps it would have been better just to ask me for my annual income and the number of kids I have, then take an estimate from there. My point is not to say these are bad. They aren't, and ultimately I'm choosing to use one to offset the emissions I can't easily eliminate on my own and all the emissions associated with publishing this book. The exercise points out how challenging all this estimation is at the lowest level. You can imagine how hard it is for a company, city, or county to do this.

The differences didn't stop there. The methods these companies offered to offset the emissions of my family varied widely. Some offered forest restoration and preservation projects. These come in a wide variety, from projects in the northeast US to the Amazon, Borneo, and places in between. Some are supplying low emission cookstoves in the developing world; others are funding renewable energy projects. Meanwhile, some just offered a bundle of less-specific projects. Some of the projects were certified by third-party verifiers, and others claimed to do their own verification. The prices offered per ton of CO_2 offset were highly variable. There was no common market for verified uniform projects that these companies were tapping into. It's a minefield. As a consumer, you are left with more questions than answers. None of it seems to scale well. For my family, these aren't overly consequential questions. For a business or government trying to spend its money wisely, make sound investments, and be accountable to shareholders, regulators, and taxpayers, the implications become more significant.

CHALLENGES OF EMISSIONS OFFSETS

Plenty has been written about emissions offsets, but some of it is not great. A lot of criticism seems fair, if perhaps premature. It's hard to imagine a path to a zero-carbon economy without putting a price on emissions and providing incentives for developing projects and technologies that sequester carbon. We also need to innovate better ways for fully valuing the stream of benefits we accrue from nature. Numerous studies have pointed out the challenges. Carbon Direct and UC Berkeley created a database of all the carbon credits that had been traded on exchanges like the European Carbon Market. Their findings state 85 percent of them have significant flaws, where the credits seem to overestimate what was sequestered, or there are difficulties verifying the programs.

There is also a bigger question about whether it's a good idea for emitters to be able to offset all their emissions. The use of cheap, plentiful, unverified offsets at the drop of a hat by some emitters, especially in the early days of the European carbon market, indeed led to much dubiety. Was it just greenwashing where rich companies and big polluters could buy their way into compliance without having to make any adjustments to their own operations? With offsets, ultimately, emissions aren't being reduced.

The offset programs themselves could be very removed from the emissions they were offsetting and have a litany of other problems. Are the projects real? Have they been verified, and is their sound science behind the verification showing the carbon calculations are plausible?

- Real—Do the projects exist?
- Verifiable—Is there some kind of third-party verification of the size, scope, and quality of the programs?
- Leakage—Does a measure, like forest preservation in one area, just lead to timbering in other areas?
- Permanence/Durability—How long does the carbon sequestration program last, and will the carbon sink be permanent?
- Additionality—Is the offset truly an additional reduction in emissions, or is it just subsidizing something that is already affordable and possible, like the deployment of solar panels?
- No-Harm/Co-Benefits—Is the offset project also producing other benefits in terms of equity or attaining other sustainable development goals?
- Enforcement—Double counting. Are the carbon credits registered and retired properly to ensure they aren't used over and over?
- Accuracy of measures—How accurate is the estimation of the sequestration or emissions avoidance? Not all bottoms-up measurements are accurate.

Despite all these challenges, there is tremendous promise in developing a set of program standards and certifications that are trusted. Carbon credit markets can help companies better transition their operations. They can provide income streams for suppliers of carbon sequestration that accelerate the preservation of our biome. Making them work is a necessary climate change mitigation solution. Current providers of these credits point out that we are in the early stages of development. The principles of action clearly apply here. You must try some things and evolve from there. There are currently several initiatives to develop and implement better standards for carbon credits.

CARBON CREDIT VERIFIERS

Into this growing market of carbon credits has come a variety of organizations attempting to create standards and best practices for carbon sequestration programs. Some companies that organize carbon management programs for companies develop and manage their own programs. Some do their own verification. Others only utilize programs that have been verified using standards designed by organizations like Verra, American Carbon Registry, or Gold Standard—the principal nonprofit organizations that create standards for offset programs. With all the challenges pointed out above, some have been quick to criticize the voluntary carbon market and the offset programs. I had a chance to speak with David Antonioli, CEO of Verra, about the evolution of carbon offsets, the development of standards, and where he thinks it's going.

David is an immensely engaging and thoughtful person. Speaking with him, he immersed me in the details of what they do and how programs and associated standards are developed, applied, and verified for various projects. Product development for them involves trying to use the best science possible to create trusted standards and monitoring procedures. Verra was born out of the international development arena, where there is a need for the verification of international development initiatives. For decades there has been a need for the United Nations, USAID, and other organizations to perform project evaluation to ensure development goals were reached. As part of the Kyoto Climate Accord, these practices were expanded. Countries with emissions reductions commitments could implement projects in developing countries. These projects could earn saleable emissions reductions credits. These would count toward the countries commitments. This was known as the Clean Development Mechanism (CDM). Under this framework, initial standards were set up to do the necessary MRV on these projects. It was early days, very early days. It was understandably inadequate and imperfect—but action was taken. Out of the need for greater independence, sophistication, and scale—Verra was born.

The reporting and procedures can be detailed to the point of being burdensome for the program providers. That's not a bad thing. The standards are rigorous in many ways. They involve detailed project design and development, ongoing reporting, and on-the-ground auditing from third parties and other measures to ensure the programs produce genuine benefits in the form of a carbon sink or the prevention of carbon emissions. This was confirmed when I spoke with Brian McFarland of CarbonFund.org. He's worked on originating and evaluating several projects. As Brian said, "I'm definitely an advocate of the standards. I think the standards do a really good job outlining a lot of requirements; the methodologies are rigorous. The independent audits are quite thorough. Of course, there are real-world complications on the ground in developing countries, but the program review, approval, and audit process is very rigorous." Yet, over the last few years, Verra and other standards organizations have come under some withering criticism that questions the validity of the programs they certify.

As I talk to David, he's very open about these issues. He believes it's part of the continued evolution and innovation of the verification standards and procedures as well as the science and technology applied to make the standards and the programs better and better. He's also adamant that the standards provide an avenue for massive conservation finance necessary to meet the climate challenge. It's still early innings. The standards need to evolve and improve, and they will. Don't throw the baby out with the bathwater. "It's about how we make the system better, more accessible, more trusted, more efficient, and affordable. We want to have more integrity in our standards and be the most trusted verification system out there."

David shared a few projects he thinks are particularly innovative and showcase the promise and benefits of the type of benefits that can be generated with financing from verified carbon credits. Dealing with the local context and trying to understand the counterfactual analysis of land use patterns to determine the additionality and permanence of these projects can be challenging. As an outsider, the detail and thoughtfulness of the projects are impressive. One project reduces deforestation in the Madre de Dios region of Peru. The project preserves a designated area and then creates a sustainable forestry project in a buffer zone around it with local community engagement and buy-in. The idea is the economic benefits in the buffer zone and enforcement will lead to better long-term sustainment of the program. It's just one example of the detailed considerations that come into the design of these projects. The potential of these programs and this form of market-based financing to help reduce GHG emissions and meet land and water conservation and other sustainable development objects is hard to deny. The stakes of getting this right are high.

There are some examples of concern from other industries, where well-intentioned verification programs may mislead users and allow companies to continue bad practices. Dolphin-safe tuna is one example. The system relies upon a significant amount of self-reporting and under-resourced attempts to track practices on the open ocean. The programs aren't rigorous, and the organizations responsible for them rely upon labeling license fees provided by the tuna producers. So, there is an inherent conflict of interest. Recent consumer climate labeling initiatives may fall into the same trap.

HERE COME THE CONSULTANTS

A variety of firms, some of whom have been working on this for many years now, are growing into the business of helping firms calculate their emissions. Carbon Direct, as we discussed in an earlier chapter, is one of these companies. They help companies identify and quantify their emissions and develop strategies for reducing and offsetting them. The list goes on: Carbon Check, Carbon Plan, and Climate Advisors. Quantified Ventures also is engaged in this in a small way. It's interesting to see the associated interest from more prominent consulting and accounting firms. Indeed, they are looking at this as a potential practice area in the future. As Eric Letsinger, CEO of Quantified Ventures, said, "I meet regularly with big-five consulting and accounting firms. I know they are interested in what's being done in this budding industry. They are waiting for an opportunity to jump in at scale." This makes sense. As the market grows, as the SEC and others develop rules for reporting on climate risks, large consulting firms, from audit practices to systems and strategy, can be expected to establish CO_2 management practices.

WE'LL GET IT STRAIGHTENED OUT—PRINCIPLES OF INNOVATION

You can see where this is going. A mainstream measurement, reporting, and verification system will be required to numerically manage GHGs in the future and keep the carbon cycle in balance. We will know this is working when it goes mainstream—and it's well on its way there already. The current push toward better ESG reporting and mainlining ESG investing and the associated metrics will lead to more standard reporting on emissions for every public company traded on a major exchange. The SEC and other market monitors will require them in the future and are already necessitating some forms of reporting. Investors will demand more as they are now. Niche firms currently provide emissions accounting, and management advisory will fold into practice areas at bulge bracket accounting and consulting firms like Deloitte, Accenture, and others. Standards of practice will be mainstreamed. Every accountant will be attending professional education conferences on how to quantify emissions budgets.

Firms will continue to offer their services to create carbon management programs for large companies. Some energy companies will become carbon management companies; the greening of industries will go mainstream. And, ultimately, trillions of dollars will be made.

CHAPTER 14

The Road Ahead

"The climate crisis is here, and the cost of inaction is already staggering."

—CONGRESSMAN FRANK PALLONE, JR. (D-N.J.)

"If you want to be successful in business (in life, actually), you have to create more than you consume. Your goal should be to create value for everyone you interact with."

—JEFF BEZOS, AMAZON 2020 LETTER TO SHAREHOLDERS

I need the juxtaposition of these two quotes to finish this book off. For starters, even as I've written and edited this book, it feels like the negative impacts of climate change are mounting. Arctic sea ice cover hit record lows. Fires raged in Siberia. Record high temperatures were set in Europe and reached nearly uninhabitable levels. Time is running short. The perils are upon us. **We should be outraged.**

Aside from fossil fuel companies, perhaps no one has more at stake than Amazon. Few companies, if any, have more impressive resources to address climate change. The prospect of quoting Jeff Bezos—one of the wealthiest people in the world and founder of a company whose carbon footprint, based on its own accounting, increased by 19 percent in 2020—might seem a bit incredulous. But Amazon, just by its sheer scale, could be a good measure of where we are right now in the climate crisis. They have acknowledged the problem publicly. Amazon has established clear goals and timelines for addressing it throughout its value chain. They are investing resources to get it done. Perhaps most importantly, I'm sure they have a strategy to make a ton of money off it.

That's actually pretty good. I have to say that's a lot better than oil company executives being taken to court and challenged in the board room or their lobbyists letting it slip that they intentionally deceived the public for decades. We've come a long way, and we have longer to go. Still, progress is underway and accelerating.

I started writing this book because I was impressed and inspired by the stories I read and people I met who were working on innovative ideas to positively impact climate change. I wanted to learn more about climate change, amplify their voice, simplify the discussion, and give all of us—including myself—more reason to take action. I also wanted to make everyone more aware of avenues for doing so. I hope I've accomplished that in some incremental way.

People like Chris Adamo, Ricardo Bayon, Kristen Rechberger, Jonathan Goldberg, David Antonielli, Tim Male, Cody Simms, and many others are part of a growing vanguard that is now a mainstream effort to mitigate climate change.

I've told these stories, but there are so many to tell, and every week there are almost countless podcasts and news articles showcasing more. They are creating new materials. They are structuring new financial models that put a value on ecosystem benefits and price on CO_2 emissions. They are developing policy and regulatory frameworks that help incentivize necessary change.

HAVE HOPE

For those who have been fighting hard for climate change for a long time, it can feel exhausting and exasperating. The facts seem simple. Why aren't we making more progress? Why haven't our political leaders taken more comprehensive action? What can I possibly do without that leadership? If you are like me or my kids and you don't spend most of your time or your professional life fighting to mitigate climate change, it's easy to think the problem is too big to solve or that there's nothing you can do. "So how, with our limited human minds, do we attend enough to make real progress? How do we not flinch and look away?" (Weil 2021).

We must have hope. Hope is a precedent to action; it's the catalyst. It's not naïve but instead backed by evidence. More and more avenues are opening for us as individuals and professionals to take singular and collective action to incrementally address the climate challenge. What is the 1 percent improvement we can make today—personally, professionally, and within our community? There are more ways today to invest our money in ways that support the path to zero-carbon emissions. There are more ways to buy the things we need for a modern life that are responsibly produced. Also, there are more ways to purchase the removal of the carbon we emit. The community we can engage with to do all these things is large and growing. We can choose to work for companies that say and do the right things on climate. We can help our current employers understand doing right by the environment is good for business. Hope drives action. Action drives innovation, which creates a future state from which more progress is possible. The wheel turns faster and faster as progress compounds.

THE MATH IS NOT COMPLICATED

The carbon cycle and our biosphere—in essence, our life support system on this spaceship—are vast and complex—and thank goodness they are! That is what makes them resilient. Complexity brings stability. Diversity brings robustness and strength. It's very easy to think the problem is intractably complex or questionable, but it's pretty simple math. To solve the problem, we must be numerical about it. We must reduce our carbon emissions by about fifty billion tons per year. We understand where that comes from—transportation, agriculture, buildings, materials, energy production, etc. For many of these areas, we already know what the mitigation strategies are. It's estimated 70–80 percent of the solutions required to meet our 2030 goals already exist at scale. About 50 percent of the solutions exist to meet our 2050 goals. For others, we need to offset them by investing in nature-based solutions to remove carbon from the atmosphere in quantities greater than what we estimate the emissions are to account for the uncertainty of the emissions and the removal. Claiming we don't understand the problem well enough to take action isn't true. It hasn't been for a long time. We need a bias toward action.

POSITIVE CHANGE IS HAPPENING AND ACCELERATING

Action creates momentum; momentum creates progress. It's not perfect. It may be inefficient. It's okay to be critical of actions taken. We need to try, evaluate, improve, and iterate. Innovation is not efficient, nor is it the time for efficiency. If we need to rework most of the economy and retool most of the built world, that process is not going to be efficient. As new systems, processes, and institutions come fully online, more efficiency can be driven into the system.

When you are close to a problem, it's easy to just see all the flaws in it. I read an article about seagrass restoration recently, and my mind was racing through all the problems. The project is so small. Storms or warming waters could wipe out the grasses again. How will they provide more funding to sustain and expand the effort? I was missing the main point. I was reading an article about seagrass restoration and climate change in the *Wall Street Journal*. That's a sign of progress. Ten years ago, ESG investing was fringe. Today, it's mainstream and doubling in size each year. Ten years ago, renewable energy projects were novel, and now they are routine and the dominant area of energy growth. The list goes on. Progress is happening and accelerating. Progress hides its tracks, and often our perspective is too close to see it. Quietly, emissions in the developing world are going down. Quietly, we are preserving more habitat. Quietly, we are decarbonizing our transportation system. We aren't doing any of it fast enough, but progress often starts slow and then ramps up as momentum builds and threshold conditions are met.

WE MUST BRING THE HEAD AND THE HEART TOGETHER

For as long as I can remember, being good to the environment has felt like a compromise. It was something we thought we should do if forced or if it happened to be the cheapest alternative. It was about something we had to give up to get what we wanted. The head said to maximize what's best for you. The heart reminded you not to forget all the nature stuff over "there." It was this extra thing we thought we needed to define the ethical grounds to support. Now—*today*—it seems clear there is no "us" or "them," no "here" or "there." There is only "we" and "here." We must reject any economic form of decision-making or organization of resources that don't rigorously and actively quantify and account for the benefits we reap from nature and the costs our actions impose on it. If we reconcile our understanding of nature as our support system on this spaceship and fully value the services we derive from it, we can create a much more prosperous future.

IF I COULD WAVE A MAGIC WAND, I WOULD

There is a lot of amazing magic out there and a lot of innovation. It's hard to pick just a few things that are on the top of my list, but here we go:

- Put a price on CO_2 everywhere I could and create fundamental markets for ecosystem services that are credible, transparent, and liquid. It will provide an incentive for mitigation strategies we can't imagine yet. Fortunately, emissions trading markets are growing everywhere. Brilliant and creative financial people are figuring out how to commodify carbon sequestration

- Stop searching for more oil and gas. Fortunately, this is rapidly becoming uneconomic. It's financial suicide for a company to spend money exploring for something that won't have any value in the future.
- Pay bottom trawlers to stop fishing, just like we pay farmers to conserve the land.
- Set aside 30 percent of the land and oceans now. Just leave them alone. Let nature do nature. Let's limit the reach of the Anthropocene.
- Accelerate the electrification of everything—transportation, heating, cooking.
- Find better ways for young people to engage and feel like they have the power to make an impact. They feel helpless. That's ominously troubling.
- As individuals, reach for that 1 percent change every day. What's the next thing I can do to have a positive impact? Okay, I don't need a magic wand for this one, and neither do you.

WE GOT THIS

All the people I have interacted with in writing this book give me hope we can do this. I'm constantly impressed with the energy, ingenuity, good nature, and heart of the people I've encountered. I'm grateful for the opportunity to learn from them and tell their stories. We should be outraged more isn't being done because so much is possible. We can do this. We must; not for nature or the earth—but for us.

I set out to write this book to learn and get closer to answering the questions I had, alongside trying to illuminate some ideas I thought were missing from the climate change debate. The debate seemed too complicated. We have been searching for one-size-fits-all solutions. We fall into the same false choice trope of caring for the environment versus maximizing the return for us. The climate crisis is portrayed as too big of a challenge to overcome. It's a hopeless cause, so why bother trying?

What I think I've learned over the last year is the opposite of this mentality is closer to the truth. The math of the planet is simple. Yes, there is variability and uncertainty, but what we know is accurate enough to be actionable. Diverse and sometimes complex and multilayered solutions are not unwelcome or to be feared. They are exactly what will make for a robust and enduring resolution to the climate crisis. We need regulatory, financial, technological, and entrepreneurial solutions—and everything in between, all at once. Conserving nature isn't a cost; it's an investment in a vast array of assets that provide a continuous and growing set of ecosystem benefits. We are only now figuring out how to value and seamlessly incorporate these assets into how we value the output of our activities. Finally, action gives us the hope of success. Every step we take to resolve the climate crisis is progress, even those that don't work. They teach us something. Every creation is a magic trick that makes the next step possible. We got this.

Acknowledgments

The term "it takes a village" has never been more vividly clear to me than at the end of this writing journey I began in January of 2021. I wouldn't have started, felt confident enough to continue, or finished it without the gracious and generous support of so many. Every time I asked for help, and many times when I didn't have the good sense to do so, you were there. You showed up with expertise, money, contacts, wisdom, encouragement, love, and most important of all, your time. I hope the finished product is half as wonderful as the support you all provided me.

I want to acknowledge all the people I interviewed for the book and who reviewed drafts and provided invaluable knowledge and expertise as I wrestled with the broad scope of this book: Chris Adamo, David, Antonioli, Ricardo Bayon, Seth Brown, Mike Check, Julia Collins, Doug Donovan, Chris Farrar, Justin Field, Jonathan Goldberg, Bryan Hanson, Phoebe Higgins, Neil Jacobs, Paula Jasinski, Randall Kempner, Jeremy Kestler, Mark Lambert, Eric Letsinger, Rebecca Letsinger, Buck Lyons, Tim Male, Kevin McAleese, Brian McFarland, Alan Miller, John Paul Moscarella, Kristin

Rechberger, Chris Rugaber, Cody Simms, Dick Strasbaugh, Ron Sznaider, Petteri Taalas, Leif Ulstrup, Eric Waeckerlin, and James Whetstone.

I'd like to thank everyone who has joined me on the journey and supported the campaign to publish the book. Your generosity and faith in me are humbling. Thank you: Mike Alberghini, Bud and Marie Anderson, Leslie Anderson, Tom Anderson, John Armstrong, Luke Astell, Felix Aygue, Apoorva Bajaj, Alison and Steve Barnes, Kurt Borcherding, Heidi Bourgeois, Mary Brabec, Bill Callahan, Matt Carlson, Gary Cecchine, Danny Christian, Jim Connolly, Bill Conway, Peter Cousins, Terry and Nina Daughenbaugh, Julie Dellinger, Susan Demske, Nick Donovan, Corinne Drumheller, Steve Dunai, Mike Eilts, Betsy Fader, John Feller, Leslie Ferry, Joanne Fischer, Heidi Fitzharris, Charles Franklin, Alan George, Alison Giffen, Jennifer Golden, Maria Greene, Mark Grovic, Emily Hanavan, Charles Harris, Todd Hinrich, Phil Hoffmann, Sven Kaiser, Jeremy Kestler, Raj Khokha, Cheh Kim, Eric Koester, John Kotnour, Rebecca Leonardi, Nancy Letsinger, Carlie Liu, Carey Lohrenz, Scott Lynch, Kumar Margasahayam, Bob Marshall, Peter Mellen, Rasean Miller, Scott Mitic, Aida Olkkonen, Randy Peale, Micaela Pond, Andy Potter, Jon Reifschneider, John Righini, Aari Roberts, Jon Rolfe, Dan Saaty, John Saaty, Steve Sapourn, Cristiana Serbanescu, Charles Solomon, Rich Spaulding, Dennis Stuart, Chuck Szymanski, Tom Thorton, Iris Trieb, John Tucker, Silvia Veitia Smith, Glenn Vogal, Jeff Walters, Rob Waschbusch, Greg Werner, Tim Wike, Todd Williams, and Pat Wolf.

I have the great fortune of living in the wonderful neighborhood of Maywood in Arlington, Virginia. So many of my neighbors and friends provided support. My classmates from the Georgetown University School of Business provided amazing support. Special thanks go to my University of Wisconsin rowing family. "We few, we happy few, we band of brothers." You showed up in so many ways. I'm inspired by you all to be a better person every day. Rawhide!

Finally, thank you to the Creator Institute, New Degree Press, and all the phenomenally talented, positive, and encouraging people who work there. I have no idea how you do it. It's like Willy Wonka's Chocolate Factory. Thank you, Linda Berardelli, Brian Bies, Amanda Brown, Eric Koester, Asa Loewenstein, Abbey Murphy, Gjorgji Pejkovski, Heather Anne Sharp, Nikola Tikoski, Kathy Wood, and many others behind the scenes who have been my wise trail guides along this journey.

Appendix

INTRODUCTION

Ellerman, A., Denny; Barbara K. Buchner. "The European Union Emissions Trading Scheme: Origins, Allocation, and Early Results." *Review of Environmental Economics and Policy.* 1, no.1 (2007): 66–87 doi:10.1093/reep/rem003

Gates, Bill. *How to Avoid a Climate Disaster: The Solutions We Have and the Breakthroughs We Need.* New York: Random House Large Print, 2021.

Guggenheim, Davis, dir. *An Inconvenient Truth.* 2006; United States: Paramount Vantage

Pinker, Steven. *Enlightenment Now: The Case for Reason, Science, Humanism and Progress.* New York: Viking, 2018

Rhodes, Joshua D. (@josdr83). "Fifteen years of fuel mixes in @ERCOT_ISO show 2020 as the year that wind finally overtook coal and solar generated enough energy to get its own

color on the chart." Twitter Post. 7:38 PM ·January 12, 2021.
https://twitter.com/joshdr83/status/1349153819066826755

Yurkevich, Vanessa. "GM Looks to Sell Only Emission-free Vehicles by 2035." *CNN*, January 29, 2021. https://edition.cnn.com/2021/01/28/business/gm-only-emission-free-cars-by-2035/index.html

PART 1: "WE'RE SCREWED" GET OVER IT

Herman, Rhett. "How Fast is the Earth Moving?" *Scientific American*, October 26, 1998. https://www.scientificamerican.com/article/how-fast-is-the-earth-mov/

Stager, C. 2012. "What Happens AFTER Global Warming?" *Nature Education Knowledge* 3 (10):7 https://www.nature.com/scitable/knowledge/library/what-happens-after-global-warming-25887608/

CHAPTER 1: THE NEED AND THE CALL TO ACTION

Buis, Alan. "The Atmosphere: Getting a Handle on Carbon Dioxide. Global Climate Change. Sizing Up Humanity's Impacts on Earth's Changing Atmosphere: A Five-Part Series. Part Two." *NASA News Global Climate Change Vital Signs of the Planet*, October 9, 2019. https://climate.nasa.gov/news/2915/the-atmosphere-getting-a-handle-on-carbon-dioxide/

Cho, Renee. "10 Climate Change Impacts That Will Affect Us All." *Columbia Climate School* (blog), December 27, 2019. https://news.climate.columbia.edu/2019/12/27/climate-change-impacts-everyone/

Crawford, Neta C. "The Defense Department is Worried about Climate Change—and also a Huge Carbon Emitter." *The Conversation*, June 12, 2019. https://theconversation.com/the-defense-department-is-worried-about-climate-change-and-also-a-huge-carbon-emitter-118017

Dunne, Daisy. "Climate Change 'Tripled Chances' of Hurricane Harvey's Record Rain. *CarbonBrief*, December 13, 2017. https://www.carbonbrief.org/climate-change-tripled-chances-hurricane-harvey-record-rain

Fey, Tina, dir. *30 Rock*. Season 2, Episode 5, "Greenzo." Aired November 8, 2007, on NBC. https://www.peacocktv.com/watch-online/tv/30-rock/6240863759978157112/seasons/2/episodes/greenzo-episode-5/4557b537-dcb2-39e9-a3b7-fe574e9b06d4

Hu, Caitlin. "A New UN Report Urges a Radical Shift in the Way We Think About Nature." *CNN*, March 16, 2021. https://www.cnn.com/2021/02/18/americas/un-report-climate-making-peace-intl/

IPCC, 2013: *Climate Change 2013: The Physical Science Basis. Contribution of Working Group I to the Fifth Assessment Report of the Intergovernmental Panel on Climate Change* [Stocker, T.F., D. Qin, G.-K. Plattner, M. Tignor, S.K. Allen, J. Boschung, A. Nauels, Y. Xia, V. Bex and P.M. Midgley (eds.)]. Cambridge University Press, Cambridge, United Kingdom, and New York, NY, USA, 1535 pp.

Mehta, Aaron. "Climate Change is Now a National Security Priority for the Pentagon." *DefenseNews*, January 27,

2021. https://www.defensenews.com/pentagon/2021/01/27/climate-change-is-now-a-national-security-priority-for-the-pentagon/

Miller, Alan; Durwood Zaelke and Stephen O. Anderson. *Cut Super Climate Pollutants Now!* Winchester: John Hunt Publishing. Changemakers Books, 2020.

Smith, Adam. "2020 US Billion-dollar Weather and Climate Disasters in Historical Context."*Climate.gov* (blog). Updated September 27, 2021. https://www.climate.gov/news-features/blogs/beyond-data/2020-us-billion-dollar-weather-and-climate-disasters-historical

US Department of Defense. *Report on Effects of a Changing Climate to the Department of Defense.* Office of the Under Secretary of Defense for Acquisition and Sustainability, January 2019. https://media.defense.gov/2019/Jan/29/2002084200/-1/-1/1/CLIMATE-CHANGE-REPORT-2019.PDF

US Global Change Research Program. *Fourth National Climate Assessment, Volume II: Impacts, Risks, and Adaptation in the United States.* Washington, DC: US Global Change Research Program, 2018. 1515 pp. DOI: 10.7930/NCA4.2018.

World Economic Forum. *The Global Risks Report 2020.* Geneva: World Economic Forum, 2020. https://www3.weforum.org/docs/WEF_Global_Risk_Report_2020.pdf

CHAPTER 2: CARBON DIOXIDE CARBON REMOVAL

IPCC SAR WG2 (1996), Watson, R.T.; Zinyowera, M.C.; and Moss, R.H. (ed.), *Climate Change 1995: Impacts, Adaptations and Mitigation of Climate Change: Scientific-Technical Analyses*, Contribution of Working Group II to the Second Assessment Report of the Intergovernmental Panel on Climate Change, Cambridge University Press, ISBN 0-521-56431-X

IPCC, 2001: Climate Change 2001: Synthesis Report. A Contribution of Working Groups I, II, and III to the Third Assessment Report of the Intergovernmental Panel on Climate Change [Watson, R.T. and the Core Writing Team (eds.)]. Cambridge University Press, Cambridge, United Kingdom, and New York, NY, USA, 398 pp.

IPCC, 2007: *Climate Change 2007: Synthesis Report. Contribution of Working Groups I, II and III to the Fourth Assessment Report of the Intergovernmental Panel on Climate Change* [Core Writing Team, Pachauri, R.K and Reisinger, A. (eds.)]. IPCC, Geneva, Switzerland, 104 pp.

IPCC, 2013: *Climate Change 2013: The Physical Science Basis. Contribution of Working Group I to the Fifth Assessment Report of the Intergovernmental Panel on Climate Change* [Stocker, T.F., D. Qin, G.-K. Plattner, M. Tignor, S.K. Allen, J. Boschung, A. Nauels, Y. Xia, V. Bex and P.M. Midgley (eds.)]. Cambridge University Press, Cambridge, United Kingdom, and New York, NY, USA, 1535 pp.

IPCC, 2021: Summary for Policymakers. In: Climate Change 2021: The Physical Science Basis. Contribution of Working Group I to the Sixth Assessment Report of the Intergovernmental

Panel on Climate Change [MassonDelmotte, V., P. Zhai, A. Pirani, S.L. Connors, C. Péan, S. Berger, N. Caud, Y. Chen, L. Goldfarb, M.I. Gomis, M. Huang, K. Leitzell, E. Lonnoy, J.B.R. Matthews, T.K. Maycock, T. Waterfield, O. Yelekçi, R. Yu, and B. Zhou (eds.)]. Cambridge University Press. In Press.

Lexico. Oxford English Dictionary. s.v. "Carbon Cycle." Accessed October 15, 2021. https://www.lexico.com/en/definition/ carbon_cycle

Neri, Valentina. "The Carbon Budget Explained: How Much CO_2 Can We Emit and Still Save the Climate? *Lifegate,* April 8, 2021. https://www.lifegate.com/carbon-budget

Oceana Europe. "Climate Change." Accessed October 15, 2021. https://europe.oceana.org/en/climate-change-0

Riebeek, Holli. "The Carbon Cycle." *NASA Earth Observatory,* June 16, 2011. https://earthobservatory.nasa.gov/features/ CarbonCycle

Wicks, Frank. "The Engineer Who Discovered Global Warming. The American Society of Mechanical Engineers." *The American Society of Mechanical Engineers,* April 29, 2020. https:// www.asme.org/topics-resources/content/the-engineer-who-discovered-global-warming

Zinke, L. "The Colours of Carbon." *Nature Reviews Earth & Environment.* 1, no. 141 (2020). https://doi.org/10.1038/s43017-020-0037-y

CHAPTER 3: THE MATH IS SIMPLE

Bezos, Jeffrey. 2020 Letter to Shareholders. *Company News,* April 15, 2021. https://www.aboutamazon.com/news/company-news/2020-letter-to-shareholders.

Friedlingstein, Pierre, et al. "Global Carbon Budget 2020." *ESSD,* 12, no. 4 (2020): 3269–3340. https://doi.org/10.5194/essd-12-3269-2020

Gates, Bill. *How to Avoid a Climate Disaster: The Solutions We Have and the Breakthroughs We Need.* New York: Random House Large Print, 2021.

Global Monitoring Laboratory. "Trends in Atmospheric Carbon Dioxide." Carbon Cycle Greenhouse Gases. Accessed October 5, 2021. http://www.esrl.noaa.gov/gmd/ccgg/trends/global.html

Hausfather, Zeke. "Analysis: Why the IPCC 1.5C Report Expanded the Carbon Budget." *CarbonBrief,* August 10, 2018. https://www.carbonbrief.org/analysis-why-the-ipcc-1-5c-report-expanded-the-carbon-budget.

United Nations Environment Programme (2019). Emissions Gap Report 2019. UNEP, Nairobi. https://wedocs.unep.org/bitstream/handle/20.500.11822/30797/EGR2019.pdf

Woellert, Lorraine, Ben Lefebvre, Kalina Oroschakoff and America Hernandez. "'Powerful Signal': In a Single Day, Big Oil Suffers Historic Blows on Climate. Courts, Customers and Wall Street Delivered Rebukes to Exxon Mobil, Chevron and Shell." *Politico,* May 27, 2021. https://www.politico.eu/article/powerful-signal-in-a-single-day-big-oil-suffers-historic-blows-on-climate/.

CHAPTER 4: WE CAN DO THIS

Aden, Nate. "The Roads to Decoupling: 21 Countries Are Reducing Carbon Emissions While Growing GDP." *World Resources Institute,* April 5, 2016. https://www.wri.org/insights/roads-decoupling-21-countries-are-reducing-carbon-emissions-while-growing-gdp.

Funk, Cary and Brian Kennedy. "How Americans See Climate Change and the Environment in 7 Charts." *Pew Research Center,* April 21, 2020. https://www.pewresearch.org/fact-tank/2020/04/21/how-americans-see-climate-change-and-the-environment-in-7-charts/

Harvey, Chelsea. "Scientists Can Now Blame Individual Natural Disasters on Climate Change. Extreme Event Attribution is One of the Most Rapidly Expanding Areas of Climate Science." *Scientific American,* January 2, 2018. https://www.scientificamerican.com/article/scientists-can-now-blame-individual-natural-disasters-on-climate-change/.

Hefferon, Meg. "Most Americans say climate change impacts their community, but effects vary by region." *Pew Research Center,* December 1. 2019. https://www.pewresearch.org/fact-tank/2019/12/02/most-americans-say-climate-change-impacts-their-community-but-effects-vary-by-region/.

Liu, P.R., Raftery, A.E. "Country-based Rate of Emissions Reductions should Increase by 80% Beyond Nationally Determined Contributions to Meet the 2 °C Target." *Commun Earth Environ* **2,** 29 (2021). https://doi.org/10.1038/s43247-021-00097-8

"Nation's Experts Give Up." *The Onion,* June 16, 1999. https://www.theonion.com/nations-experts-give-up-1819565216.

Newburger, Emma. "Climate Change has Cost the US Billions of Dollars in Flood Damage, Study Finds." *CNBC,* January 11, 2021. https://www.cnbc.com/2021/01/11/climate-change-has-cost-the-us-billions-of-dollars-in-flood-damage.html.

Nichols, Tom. *The Death of Expertise.* New York, NY: Oxford University Press, 2018.

Science Based Targets Initiative. *Home Page.* AMBITIOUS CORPORATE CLIMATE ACTION. Accessed October 5, 2021. https://sciencebasedtargets.org/.

Thaler, Richard. *Misbehaving: The Making of Behavioral Economics.* New York: W.W. Norton and Company Ltd, 2015.

UNFCCC. "Most Developed Countries on Track to Meet their 2020 Emission Reduction Targets, but More Ambition Needed by Some." *United Nations Climate Change News,* November 23, 2020. https://unfccc.int/news/most-developed-countries-on-track-to-meet-their-2020-emission-reduction-targets-but-more-ambition.

UNFCCC. *Join the Race.* Race to Zero & Race to Resilience. Accessed October 5, 2021. https://racetozero.unfccc.int/join-the-race/.

PART 2: PRINCIPLES THAT GET US THERE

Simms, Cody and Clay Dumas. "Breakthrough Climate Technologies with Clay Dumas." March 24, 2021. In *Techstars Climate Tech Podcast*. Produced by Cody Simms. Podcast, MP3 Audio, 32 min. https://www.techstars.com/the-line/podcasts/breakthrough-climate-technologies-with-clay-dumas.

CHAPTER 5: THE SCIENCE OF A BIAS TOWARD ACTION

Bar-Eli, M., O.H Azar., I. Ritov, Y. Keidar-Levin, , and G. Schein. "Action Bias Among Elite Soccer Goalkeepers: The Case of Penalty Kicks." *Journal of Economic Psychology*. 28, no. 5 (2007): 606–621. DOI: 10.1016/j.joep.2006.12.001

Clear, James. *Atomic Habits: An Easy & Proven Way to Build Good Habits & Break Bad Ones ; Tiny Changes, Remarkable Results*. New York: Avery, an imprint of Penguin Random House, 2018.

Encyclopedia Britannica Online. s.v. "Newton's laws of motion." Accessed on October 6, 2021, https://www.britannica.com/science/Newtons-laws-of-motion.

Figueres, Christiana. "The Inside Story of the Paris Climate Agreement." Filmed February 2016. TED2016 video, 2:55 and 4:15. https://www.ted.com/talks/christiana_figueres_the_inside_story_of_the_paris_climate_agreement.

Ishii, Naoko. "An Economic Case for Protecting the Environment." Filmed September 2017 at TEDGlobal NYC. TED video, 6:35. https://www.ted.com/talks/naoko_ishii_an_economic_case_for_protecting_the_planet

National Academies of Sciences, Engineering, and Medicine. 2016. *Attribution of Extreme Weather Events in the Context of Climate Change.* Washington, DC: The National Academies Press. https://doi.org/10.17226/21852.

O'Hanlon, Ryan. "Everyone is Bad at Shooting," *No Grass In The Clouds,* December 17, 2019. https://nograssintheclouds. substack.com/p/everyone-is-bad-at-shooting.

Peters, Tom. "A Bias for Action." May 20, 2016. Video, 5:51. https://www.youtube.com/watch?v=ooLoBPsjFgw.

Thaler, Richard. *Misbehaving: The Making of Behavioral Economics.* W.W. Norton and Company Ltd, New York, NY. 2015.

"Why Do We Prefer doing Something to Doing Nothing? The Action Bias, Explained." *The Decision Lab.* Accessed: October 6, 2021. https://thedecisionlab.com/biases/action-bias/.

CHAPTER 6: PRINCIPLES OF INNOVATION

Caroli, Paulo. March 24, 2016. "The Technology Adoption Curve." *Caroli.org* (blog), March 24, 2016. https://www.caroli.org/en/the-technology-adoption-curve/.

Elkington, John. *Green Swans. The Coming Boom in Regenerative Capitalism.* New York: Fast Company Press, 2020.

Furr, Nathan and Jeff Dyer. "Choose the Right Innovation Method at the Right Time." *Harvard Business Review,* December 31, 2014. https://hbr.org/2014/12/choose-the-right-innovation-method-at-the-right-time.

Hudson, Dr. Ken. "What is the Best Definition of Innovation?" *Dr. Ken Hudson*, March 13, 2014. https://drkenhudson.com/best-way-define-innovation/.

Jacobs, Jason and Mary Powell. "Episode 162: Mary Powell, Clean Energy Leader & Former CEO of Green Mountain Power." June 8th, 2021. In *My Climate Journey*. Podcast, MP3 audio, 13:30. https://www.myclimatejourney.co/episodes/mary-powell.

Leong, Kathy Chin. "Google Reveals Its 9 Principles of Innovation." *Fast Company*, November 20, 2013. https://www.fastcompany.com/3021956/googles-nine-principles-of-innovation.

Moore, Geoffrey A. *Crossing the Chasm: Marketing and Selling Technology Products to Mainstream Customers*. New York: HarperBusiness, 1991.

Taleb, Nassim Nicholas. *The Black Swan. The Impact of the Highly Improbable*. New York: Random House, 2007.

CHAPTER 7: WE NEED MORE WAYS TO PLUG MONEY INTO THIS

Klebnikov, Sergei. "Stopping Global Warming Will Cost $50 Trillion: Morgan Stanley Report." *Forbes,* October 24, 2019. https://www.forbes.com/sites/sergeiklebnikov/2019/10/24/stopping-global-warming-will-cost-50-trillion-morgan-stanley-report/?sh=7a8a301551e2.

Koester, Eric and Scott Harris. "Interview with Scott Harris." March 15, 2021. In *Never Write Alone*. Podcast, MP3 audio.

Rand, Tom. *The Case for Climate Capitalism—Economic Solutions for Climate Change*. Toronto: ECW Press, 2020.

The World Bank. "GDP (US$) World Bank national accounts data, and OECD National Accounts data files." Accessed October 7, 2021. https://data.worldbank.org/indicator/NY.GDP.MKTP.CD.

CHAPTER 8: REGULATION PLAYS A BIG ROLE

Bianco, Nicholas, Frank Litz, Devashree Saha, Tyler Clevenger and Dan Lashof. "New Climate Federalism: Defining Federal, State and Local Roles in a US Policy Framework to Achieve Decarbonization." *World Resources Institute*, October 2020. https://files.wri.org/d8/s3fs-public/new-climate-federalism-working-paper.pdf.

The Climate 21 Project. *Home Page*. Accessed October 8, 2021. https://climate21.org/.

Hultman, Nathan, Joseph W. Kane, and Fred Dews. "Proposals for US Climate Leadership and Managing Built Environment Risks and Costs." March 12, 2021. In *Brookings Cafeteria Podcast*. Produced by The Brookings Institution. Podcast. MP3 audio, 41:17. https://www.brookings.edu/podcast-episode/proposals-for-us-climate-leadership-and-managing-built-environment-risks-and-costs/.

Kane, Joseph W., Jenny Schuetz, Shalini Vajjhala, and Adie Tomer. "How a Federal Climate Planning Unit Can Manage Built Environment Risks and Costs." *The Brookings Institution*, March 1, 2021. https://www.brookings.edu/research/how-a-federal-climate-planning-unit-can-manage-built-environment-risks-and-costs/

UNFCCC. *Join the Race.* Race to Zero & Race to Resilience. Accessed October 5, 2021. https://racetozero.unfccc.int/join-the-race/.

Van Winkle, Christina. "Colorado's Climate Action Plan and Climate Change Data Collection." State of Colorado, Legislative Council Staff. Issue Brief, Number 20-23, November 2020. https://leg.colorado.gov/sites/default/files/r20-1191_issue_brief_on_climate_change_legislation.pdf

CHAPTER 9: GREEN CARBON

Abbott, Chuck. "'You Cannot Do Climate on the Backs of the American Farmer.'" *Successful Farming*, February 22, 2021. https://www.agriculture.com/news/business/you-cannot-do-climate-on-the-backs-of-the-american-farmer.

Feldman, Amy. July 19, 2021, 7:30 AM EDT. "Pivot Bio Nears $2 Billion Valuation As It Raises Whopping $430 Million To Replace Synthetic Fertilizers On Corn And Wheat." Forbes Magazine. https://www.forbes.com/sites/amyfeldman/2021/07/19/pivot-bio-nears-2-billion-valuation-as-it-raises-whopping-430-million-to-replace-synthetic-fertilizers-on-corn-and-wheat-sustainability/?sh=682c04a92273.

Gullickson, Guy. "How Carbon May Become Another Crop for Farmers." *Successful Farmer*, February 4, 2021. https://www.agriculture.com/farm-management/programs-and-policies/how-carbon-may-become-another-crop-for-farmers.

Kaplan, Sarah. "Humanity's Greatest Ally Against Climate Change is Earth Itself." *Washington Post,* April 22, 2021. https://www.washingtonpost.com/climate-solutions/2021/04/22/earth-day-biodiversity/.

Popkin, Gabriel. "Is carbon sequestration on farms actually working to fight climate change?" *GreenBiz,* April 15, 2020. https://www.greenbiz.com/article/carbon-sequestration-farms-actually-working-fight-climate-change.

Reiley, Laura. "USDA Secretary of Agriculture Nominee Tom Vilsack Clears First Hurdle, Says He will Focus on Climate Change." *Washington Post,* February 2, 2021. https://www.washingtonpost.com/business/2021/02/02/vilsack-usda-confirmation-hearing/.

UNFCCC. May 6, 2021. "Global Assessment: Urgent Steps Must Be Taken to Reduce Methane Emissions This Decade." External Press Release. https://unfccc.int/news/global-assessment-urgent-steps-must-be-taken-to-reduce-methane-emissions-this-decade.

United States Department of Agriculture. "US Gross Cash Farm Income Expected to Increase in 2021." *Economic Research Service.* Accessed October 9, 2021. https://www.ers.usda.gov/data-products/chart-gallery/gallery/chart-detail/?chartId=76943.

United States Department of Agriculture. September 29, 2021. "USDA Announces $3 Billion Investment in Agriculture, Animal Health, and Nutrition; Unveils New Climate Partnership Initiative, Requests Public Input." https://www.usda.gov/

media/press-releases/2021/09/29/usda-announces-3-billion-investment-agriculture-animal-health-and.

United States Senate Committee on Agriculture, Nutrition & Forestry. "2014 Farm Bill." February 4th, 2014. https://www.agriculture.senate.gov/issues/farm-bill.

CHAPTER 10: BLUE CARBON

Alongi, Daniel M. "Carbon Cycling and Storage in Mangrove Forests." *Annual Review of Marine Science*, 6 (2014): 195–219. https://doi.org/10.1146/annurev-marine-010213-135020.

Benveniste, Alexis. "This Startup Grows Kelp then Sinks it to Pull Carbon from the Air," *CNN Business*, May 3, 2021. https://www.cnn.com/2021/05/03/business/running-tide-kelp-carbon/index.html.

Carlyle, Ryan. "Why Don't We Spend More On Exploring The Oceans, Rather Than On Space Exploration?" *Forbes*, January 13, 2013. https://www.forbes.com/sites/quora/2013/01/31/why-dont-we-spend-more-on-exploring-the-oceans-rather-than-on-space-exploration/?sh=54c7af7f2ed3.

Chami, Ralph, Thomas Cosimano, Connel Fullenkamp, and Sena Oztosun. December 2019. "Nature's Solution to Climate Change." *Finance and Development* 56, no. 4 (December 2019). https://www.imf.org/external/pubs/ft/fandd/2019/12/natures-solution-to-climate-change-chami.htm.

Development News. "'Nature-based solutions': Biodiversity Saving the Climate." *iD4D*. Updated January 20, 2020.

https://ideas4development.org/en/nature-based-solutions-biodiversity-saving-the-climate/.

Einhorn, Catrin. "Trawling for Fish May Unleash as Much Carbon as Air Travel, Study Says." *New York Times*, March 17, 2021. https://www.nytimes.com/2021/03/17/climate/climate-change-oceans.html.

Esgro, Mike. "North Coast Kelp Forest Restoration Project Showing Early Evidence of Success." *California Natural Resources Agency*, September 18, 2020. https://resources.ca.gov/Newsroom/Page-Content/News-List/North-Coast-Kelp-Forest-Restoration-Project-Showing-Early-Evidence-of-Success.

Fothergill, Alastair, Jonathan Hughes, Keith Scholey, dirs. *A Life on Our Planet;* 2020. Los Gatos, CA: Netflix.

Fredriksen, S., K. Filbee-Dexter, K.M. Norderhaug, H. Steen, T. Bodvin, M.A. Coleman, F. Moy, T. Wernberg. "Green Gravel: A Novel Restoration Tool to Combat Kelp Forest Decline." *Scientific Reports* 10, no. 3983 (2020). https://doi.org/10.1038/s41598-020-60553-x.

Gibbens, Sarah. "The World Has Two Years to Meet Marine Protection Goal. Can It Be Done?" *National Geographic*, March 2, 2018. https://www.nationalgeographic.com/science/article/marine-protected-areas-assessment-environment-conservation-spd.

Griscom, Bronson W., Justin Adams, Peter W. Ellis, Richard A. Houghton, Guy Lomax, Daniela A. Miteva, William H.

Schlesinger, David Shoch, Juha V. Siikamäki, Pete Smith, Peter Woodbury, Chris Zganjar, Allen Blackman, João Campari, Richard T. Conant, Christopher Delgado, Patricia Elias, Trisha Gopalakrishna, Marisa R. Hamsik, Mario Herrero, Joseph Kiesecker, Emily Landis, Lars Laestadius, Sara M. Leavitt, Susan Minnemeyer, Stephen Polasky, Peter Potapov, Francis E. Putz, Jonathan Sanderman, Marcel Silvius, Eva Wollenberg, Joseph Fargione. "Natural Climate Solutions." *Proceedings of the National Academy of Sciences*, 114, no. 44 (October 2017): 11645–11650. DOI: 10.1073/pnas.1710465114

Hoegh-Guldberg, Ove, Eliza Northrop, Joyashree Roy, Mansi Konar and Jane Lubchenco. "Turning the Tide: Ocean-Based Solutions Could Close Emission Gap by 21%." *World Resources Institute,* September 23, 2019. https://www.wri.org/insights/turning-tide-ocean-based-solutions-could-close-emission-gap-21.

Jones, Nicola. "Why the Market for 'Blue Carbon' Credits May Be Poised to Take Off." *YaleEnvironment360*, April 13, 2021. https://e360.yale.edu/features/why-the-market-for-blue-carbon-credits-may-be-poised-to-take-off.

Kaplan, Sarah. "Humanity's greatest ally against climate change is Earth itself." *Washington Post*, April 22, 2021. https://www.washingtonpost.com/climate-solutions/2021/04/22/earth-day-biodiversity/.

Katija K, and JO Dabiri. "A Viscosity-enhanced Mechanism for Biogenic Ocean Mixing." *Nature* 460, no. 7255 (July 2009): 624-6. DOI: 10.1038/nature08207.

Kershner, Kate. "Do we really know more about space than the deep ocean?" *How Stuff Works*, April 27, 2021. https://science. howstuffworks.com/environmental/earth/oceanography/ deep-ocean-exploration.htm.

Krause-Jensen, Dorte and Carlos M. Duarte. "Substantial Role of Macroalgae in Marine Carbon Sequestration." *Nature Geoscience* 9 (September 2016). DOI: 10.1038/NGEO2790.

Marine Bio. *Did You Know . . .? Marine Life/Ocean Facts.* Marine Life. Accessed October 9, 2021. https://www.marinebio.org/ creatures/facts/.

Muth, Arley F., Michael H. Graham, Christopher E. Lane and Christopher D. G. Harley. "Recruitment Tolerance to Increased Temperature Present Across Multiple Kelp Clades." *Ecology Ecological Society of America* 100, no. 3 (March 2019.) https:// doi.org/10.1002/ecy.2594.

"New Report Outlines Path to Net-zero Aviation in 2050." *CANSO*, May 10, 2021. https://canso.org/new-report-outlines-path-to-net-zero-aviation-in-2050/.

NOAA. What is eutrophication? National Ocean Service. October 5, 2017. https://oceanservice.noaa.gov/facts/phyto.html

Sala, E., Enric Sala, Juan Mayorga, Darcy Bradley, Reniel B. Cabral, Trisha B. Atwood, Arnaud Auber, William Cheung, Christopher Costello, Francesco Ferretti, Alan M. Friedlander, Steven D. Gaines, Cristina Garilao, Whitney Goodell, Benjamin S. Halpern, Audra Hinson, Kristin Kaschner, Kathleen Kesner-Reyes, Fabien Leprieur, Jennifer McGowan,

Lance E. Morgan, David Mouillot, Juliano Palacios-Abrantes, Hugh P. Possingham, Kristin D. Rechberger, Boris Worm & Jane Lubchenco. "Protecting the Global Ocean for Biodiversity, Food and Climate." *Nature* 592, (2021): 397–402. https://doi.org/10.1038/s41586-021-03371-z

TEDx Talks. "Transparency Can Save the Oceans." September 6, 2018. Video, 13:31. https://www.youtube.com/watch?v=yJfKn_fNBGk.

CHAPTER 11: BLACK CARBON

Crocker, Tom, Luke Fletcher, Jinxi Chen and Alice Newman. "Melting Pot—Which Steel Companies are Ready for the Low-carbon Transition?" *CDP*, July 2019. https://6fefcbb86e61af1b2fc4-c70d8ead6ced550b4d987d7c03fcddid.ssl.cf3.rackcdn.com/cms/reports/documents/000/004/659/original/CDP_Steel_2019_Executive_summary.pdf?1564490803.

Fan, Zhiyuan, Dr. Julio Friedmann. "Low-Carbon Production of Iron & Steel: Technology Options, Economic Assessment, and Policy." *Columbia SIPA, Center on Global Energy Policy*, March 8, 2021. https://www.energypolicy.columbia.edu/research/article/low-carbon-production-iron-steel-technology-options-economic-assessment-and-policy.

Gates, Bill. *How to Avoid a Climate Disaster: The Solutions We Have and the Breakthroughs We Need.* New York: Random House Large Print, 2021.

Gearino, Dan. "Inside Clean Energy: A Steel Giant Joins a Growing List of Companies Aiming for Net-Zero by 2050." *Inside Climate News,* October 8, 2020. https://insideclimatenews.org/news/08102020/inside-clean-energy-steel-net-zero/.

Greentown Labs. "The Carbon to Value Initiative Announces First Cohort of Carbontech Startup Participants." *Cision PR Newswire,* April 28, 2021. https://www.prnewswire.com/news-releases/the-carbon-to-value-initiative-announces-first-cohort-of-carbontech-startup-participants-301278767.html.

Swisher, Kara. "Goodbye, Twitter Trump! And Other Predictions for 2021." *New York Times,* December 31, 2020. https://www.nytimes.com/2020/12/31/opinion/tech-predictions-2021.html.

Techstars. "Material Evolution | Techstars Sustainability Summit Startup Demo." April 16, 2021. Video, 4:01. https://www.youtube.com/watch?v=ndORAMPkmYE&list=PLbMZj2MrUb5zAW4xVw4Xp7w322fVpo-rl&index=17.

Techstars. "Techstars Sustainability Summit: Fireside Chat with Nicole Systrom." April 16, 2021. Video, 18:30. https://www.youtube.com/watch?v=aF0AsdC2Vw4.

Techstars. "Techstars Sustainability Summit: Opening with Maëlle Gavet, Techstars CEO." April 16, 2021. Video, 15:35. https://www.youtube.com/watch?v=FwRv_AYQK2Q.

CHAPTER 12: GOLD CARBON

BlackRock. "Sustainability at BlackRock—Our 2020 Sustainability Actions." Accessed on October 10, 2021. https://www.blackrock. com/corporate/about-us/our-2020-sustainability-actions.

BlackRocksBigProblem. *Home Page.* Accessed October 10, 2021. https://blackrocksbigproblem.com/.

Bloomberg Intelligence. "ESG Assets May Hit $53 Trillion by 2025, a Third of Global AUM." *Bloomberg Professional Services,* February 23, 2021. https://www.bloomberg.com/ professional/blog/esg-assets-may-hit-53-trillion-by-2025-a-third-of-global-aum/.

Fink, Larry. "Larry Fink's 2021 letter to CEOs." *BlackRock.* Accessed October 10, 2021. https://www.blackrock.com/us/ individual/2021-larry-fink-ceo-letter.

Iacurci, Greg. "Climate Funds Hold Less than 1% of 401(k) Money. Here's Why." *CNBC,* December 14, 2020. https:// www.cnbc.com/2020/12/11/heres-why-401k-plans-lag-in-green-investment-options.html.

Iacurci, Greg. "Money Invested in ESG Funds more than Doubles in a Year." *CNBC,* February 11, 2021. https:// www.cnbc.com/2021/02/11/sustainable-investment-funds-more-than-doubled-in-2020-.html.

Jacobes, Jason, and Jigar Shah. "Episode 76: Jigar Shah, President & Co-Founder at Generate Capital" January 30, 2020. In *My Climate Journey.* Podcast. MP3 audio, 1:03:38. https://www. myclimatejourney.co/episodes/jigar-shah.

Orsagh, Matt. "Research Reports—Climate Change Analysis in the Investment Process." *CFA Institute,* September 2021. https://www.cfainstitute.org/en/research/industry-research/climate-change-analysis.

Techstars. "Techstars Sustainability Summit: Fireside Chat with Nicole Systrom." April 16, 2021. Video, 18:29. https://www.youtube.com/watch?v=aFoAsdC2Vw4.

CHAPTER 13: ESTIMATION AND VERIFICATION

Bell, Heather. "John Kerry Backing Carbon ETF." *Daily ETF Watch,* July 31, 2020. https://www.etf.com/sections/daily-etf-watch/kerry-backing-carbon-etf?ts=1623208439.

Chestney, Nina. "Global Carbon Markets Value Surged to Record \$277 Billion Last Year—Refinitiv." *Reuters,* January 27, 2021. https://www.reuters.com/article/us-europe-carbon/global-carbon-markets-value-surged-to-record-277-billion-last-year-refinitiv-idUSKBN29W1HR.

ETF. "Carbon Credits ETF Overview." *Carbon Credits ETF Channel.* Accessed October 11, 2021. https://www.etf.com/channels/carbon-credits-etfs.

NASDAQ Press Release. "Nasdaq Acquires Emerging Carbon Removal Market Puro.earth." *NASDAQ,* June 1, 2021. https://www.nasdaq.com/press-release/nasdaq-acquires-emerging-carbon-removal-market-puro.earth-2021-06-01-0.

NIST. *James Whetstone (Fed).* People. Accessed October 11, 2021. https://www.nist.gov/people/james-whetstone.

Rowling, Megan. "Climate Primer: What is 'Net Zero' and Why Does it Matter?" *Thomson Reuters Foundation News*, May 18, 2021. https://news.trust.org/item/20200921201510-2m3lp/.

Yadav, Vineet & S, Ghosh, K. Mueller, A. Karion, G. Roest, S. M. Gourdji, I. Lopez Coto, K. Gurney, N. Parazoo, K. Verhulst, J. Kim, S. Prinzivalli, C. Fain, T. Nehrkorn, M. Mountain, R. Keeling, R. Weiss, R. Duren, C. Miller, J. Whetstone, "The Impact of COVID-19 on CO 2 Emissions in the Los Angeles and Washington DC/Baltimore Metropolitan Areas." *Geophysical Research Letters* 48, no. 11 (2021). https://doi.org/10.1029/2021GL092744

CHAPTER 14: THE ROAD AHEAD

Bezos, Jeffrey. 2020 Letter to Shareholders. *Company News*, April 15, 2021. https://www.aboutamazon.com/news/company-news/2020-letter-to-shareholders.

Mufson, Steven and Tony Romm. "As the Largest-ever US Climate Bill Inches Forward, a Lobbying Frenzy Ensues." *Washington Post*, September 13, 2021. https://www.washingtonpost.com/climate-environment/2021/09/13/budget-reconciliation-bill-climate/.

Weil, Elizabeth. "The Climate Crisis Is Worse Than You Can Imagine. Here's What Happens If You Try." *ProPublica*, January 25, 2021. https://www.propublica.org/article/the-climate-crisis-is-worse-than-you-can-imagine-heres-what-happens-if-you-try?utm_medium=social&utm_source=facebook&fbclid=IwARoh-cnM3H2uDV6JGAOXyon no72JSrx242TWthMPiLSERnNIn_Cu-sopQCA.

Endnotes

———

1   This doesn't line up exactly with the chart above, which shows about forty billion metric tons. forty billion metric tons is about forty-four billion tons. These are 2020 estimates where global emissions dipped by about 5 percent. Other references put the number at fifty-one billion tons, so I settled at the round number of fifty (Gates 2021).